# THE FATHER'S CUP

# THE FATHER'S CUP

## The Lamb Who Was Slain is Worthy to Receive the Reward of His Suffering

SANDY D. KIRK, PHD

ISBN (Paperback) : 979-8-9868-037-3-9
ISBN (eBook): 979-8-9868037-2-2

Designed by Christy Day, Constellation Books Services

Published by BEHOLD THE LAMB PUBLICATIONS

# Dedication

**This book is dedicated to all who long to bring Jesus, the Lamb who was slain, the reward of His sacrifice.**

# Contents

Introduction

# Do You Tremble?

## *Have You Looked into the Cup?*

In the stillness of a moonlit garden, under the gnarled branches of olive trees, a lone figure cries out in prayer. Who is this one who agonizes on His face in a garden of crushed olives? I'm sure you know—It's Jesus Christ, the Son of God. On the eve of His greatest sacrifice in life, He prays: *"Father . . . if you are willing, remove* ***this CUP*** *from Me."*

*This Cup?* What is this Cup, which causes Jesus to weep and wail in prayer? Do you know? The answer is fathomless, and if you will look into the depths of this Cup, your heart will never stop trembling.

The email I received from a lady in Beijing, China illustrates what I mean. She wrote asking me if she could translate this book, *The Father's Cup,* into Mandarin Chinese. Of course, I said, "Yes!" A few months later she wrote me back, saying, "From the moment I started translating, my heart trembled. I continued to shake until I finished the last sentence of the book."[1]

I wept when I read her words because this same deep inner trembling happened to me as well. God first used Jonathan Edwards, one of America's greatest theologians, to open my eyes. When I saw in the Scriptures what was in this Cup, it was like a theological revolution exploded within me. And now, forty years later, the passion has never dimmed. Best of all, beyond my wildest expectations, I've seen it happen to so many others.

I've seen students, evangelists, and pastors weeping over the Father's Cup in the wet grass of our prayer garden or on the smooth floor of our chapel in Alabama. Leaders and young people of all ages have sobbed on the dirt floors of Africa, on the carpets of England or Germany, on the ornate rugs of Hong Kong or Taiwan or Indonesia. But always it was the Cup that gripped them. Many of them testified that God had carved within them a wound of love for Jesus. To this day they tell me they still feel the love wound throbbing in their hearts. It came from looking deeply at the Cross until they saw Jesus engulfing the Father's Cup.

So, I offer you now this little book. In these pages we will peer into an olive orchard on a hill outside Jerusalem. Then we will climb another hill called Calvary[2] to behold the Lamb of God like you've never seen Him before.[3] When you see Him drinking the Father's Cup, your heart will surely tremble, not with fear, but with a living, breathing, undying holy passion for God. Come look again, for the very first time, at Jesus Christ as He engulfs every burning drop of *the Father's Cup.*[4]

Let's peek again through the olive leaves into the Garden of Gethsemane, which means "garden of crushed olives."

But what is this?

What is happening to Jesus as He thrashes wildly in prayer? What is this dark wet substance drenching His hair and dripping down His face?

## One

# A Blood-Soaked Prayer

### *When Jesus Looked into the Cup*

Silvery olive leaves shimmer in the soft spring breeze, reflecting the glow of the full Passover moon. The light flickers through the branches, shining down on Jesus. Look closely and you will see pools of something dark and red puddling around His face. Such passion and pain explode from His heart that the blood of His own vessels squeezes out through the pores of His skin.

On the night before His infinite sacrifice, this is the most profound prayer Jesus ever prayed on earth. The monumental significance of His plea stuns our senses. It is a prayer between God and God. Our eternal salvation depends on it. It is a prayer soaked in His own blood.

## POOLS OF CLOTTED BLOOD

This is the first issue of Lamb's blood, drawn from His veins without whip, or thorn, or spike to cut through His human flesh. Blood presses out through His skin like oil pressed out of an olive. Dark red clots saturate His robe: *"And being in agony, He was praying very fervently; and His sweat became like drops of blood, falling down upon the ground"* (Lk 22:44).

The Greek translation of ***"drops** of blood"* is *thrombos.* According to Greek scholar W. E. Vine, *thrombos* means "large, thick drops of clotted blood."[5] And though some dismiss this as merely heavy drops of sweat, this would be impossible, for sweat never congeals to form clots. Only blood thickens when air hits it. This could be nothing else but rich, red human blood, issuing from the veins of the Lamb.

Jonathan Edwards explained, "The distress and anguish of His mind was so unspeakably extreme as to force His blood through the pores of His skin . . , so plentifully as to fall in great clots or drops."[6] Charles Spurgeon, known as England's Prince of Preachers, said, "He not only sweat blood, but it was in great drops of blood coagulated and formed in large masses." It formed "gouts—big heavy drops," falling to the ground.[7]

## WHY SUCH ANGUISH?

Do you know of any other time when Jesus prayed so fervently that blood gushed from His pores and saturated his garments?

Never. But why? Why was blood streaming from His veins and drenching His hair and face and robe? What could evoke such fear, even horror, within Him? Do you know?

Was it knowing that soon a Roman scourge would rip His flesh to shreds? Was it His dread of long spikes piercing through His hands and feet? Was it the shame and grief He was soon to bear? Could it have been the sorrow He would feel from the rejection of those He loved? Was He simply afraid to die?

Oh no! It was so much more.

Listen again to His prayer and you will know: *"Abba! Father! All things are possible for You; remove* ***this cup*** *from me; yet not what I will but what You will"* (Mark 14:36).

What is so overwhelming about this Cup that it arouses such a violent physiological reaction? What does He see in this Cup that fills him with such horror?

Whatever it is, Spurgeon said, "It was something inconceivably terrible, amazingly full of dread, which came from the Father's hand.[8] British pastor, Arthur Pink said, "His heart was melted like wax at the sight of the terrible Cup."[9]

But what is *this Cup?* I had never heard a sermon or read a book about it, and yet Edwards said that Jesus' primary purpose, the "principal errand" He came to accomplish on earth was to drink that Cup![10] If this is true, why had I heard nothing about it? I had to know. I hope you feel the same because it is crucial to understanding the complete gospel. And though I've told my story in other books, let me tell you once more about this defining moment in my life.

## UNDONE BY THE FATHER'S CUP

One spring morning, I sat quietly in a Sunday School class, my heart in my throat, as the class tried to answer a young man's probing question: "What's the big deal about the Cross?" he asked. "Thousands have died on crosses, and we don't worship them!"

The class tried to answer his question, but nothing seemed to satisfy him. My heart yearned to tell what I had recently discovered about the Father's Cup, which is the high point of the Cross. But because I was a visitor, I felt like I should try to hold back.

As a young Bible teacher, my pastor had challenged me to read the works of Jonathan Edwards. I had devoured Edwards' writings, but when I came to a sermon entitled "Christ's Agony," it was like a spiritual grenade struck my theological foundation.[11]

Edwards said the chief reason Jesus came to earth was to drink the Father's Cup. *The Father's Cup?* I had never even heard of it. Was this a new revelation? As I continued to study, I realized this was *not* a new revelation at all. It's all through the Bible; I had simply overlooked it. I didn't know that I didn't know, and soon I found that most others didn't know either.[12] In my wildest dreams I could never have imagined the astonishing impact the Father's Cup would have on me and so many others.

As I sat there in that little Methodist Sunday School class, finally I could no longer hold back. I raised my hand and said,

"I know I'm just a visitor, but may I tell you what I've been learning about the Cross from Scripture and from Jonathan Edwards, the father of America's First Great Awakening?" The class nodded with interest.

My voice vibrated and my heart pounded hard as I tried to put it into words. I couldn't sit, so I stood and began pouring out my heart about the Father's Cup. As I spoke, the Holy Spirit began filling the room, and we were all gripped by Jesus' amazing sacrifice.

I took a deep breath and said, "The Father in heaven tore His only Son from His side and sent Him down to us as an innocent Lamb. Like a lamb, His flesh was skinned and flayed in pieces by the Roman flagellum with its bits of sharp bone and metal. His hands and feet were spiked up to a crossbeam and He hung there, naked and bearing our shame.

"But it wasn't just the physical pain and shame. It was the spiritual agony, for then His Father gathered up all our sin—yours and mine and the whole world's sin—and poured it into Him. He writhed in anguish under the filth of human sin, tearing open the wounds on His back. And then . . . came the most crucial part of the Cross. This was the apex, the pinnacle, the mountain peak of it all. This is the part we usually overlook because it's too terrible to even imagine."

I paused and tried to steady myself as I continued. "And then God His Father removed His presence and poured the full blazing contents of His Cup down upon the innocent Lamb of God. Wave after wave after wave of raw punishment roared down upon the Son until He could not bear another moment.

"Finally, after nearly three hours of unspeakable torture, Jesus pushed down on the spike in His feet to fill His lungs with air. Then He bellowed out the saddest, most horrific cry ever heard in heaven or earth.

"With all the passion and pain within Him . . . in a deep guttural, animal-like roar, He wailed, ***'My God, My God, why have You forsaken Me?'"***

I couldn't say another word. I simply sat down, bowed my head, and quietly wept.

The class was stunned, but most of all—I was completely undone. I tried to swallow my emotions as I walked into the sanctuary for the church service. As I sat there, trying to listen to Pastor Charles, my face burned and my whole being trembled. I remember thinking, *I've been baptized in the Holy Spirit for almost twenty years, but I have never felt* ***fire*** *like this! This must be what John the Baptist meant when He said, "He will baptize you with the* ***Holy Spirit and fire"*** (Luke 3:16).

My heart raced, and, like Moses when he drew near and looked at the blazing bush, it almost seemed like I should remove the shoes from my feet. Even today, forty years later, as I tell about it, I can still feel the heat on my face and the shaking inside.

As I sat in the pew, I kept thinking about all the other biblical subjects I had taught through the years. These were good Christian subjects, but they were peripheral. Like a candle in the light of the sun, they didn't compare with the fire and glory of the Cross and the Father's Cup. So right there in that large Methodist church, I repented with soul-shaking tears of godly grief for all the years I had spent teaching other subjects. I quietly sobbed in repentance for not embracing the Cross and the Father's Cup sooner.

Finally, I lifted my tear-streaked face to heaven and promised God that, for the rest of my life, I would teach and write and meditate and preach about the Cross and the Cup Jesus drank. Like the Apostle Paul, *"I determined to know nothing . . . except Jesus Christ and him crucified"* (I Cor. 2:2).

After this, everything changed. My whole being came alive with Resurrection life. I was filled with a new purpose and passion for God like I never dreamed possible. That happened decades ago, and it remains the defining moment of my Christian life. The Scriptures began to open to me as never before, and I have lived in the glow of the Cross ever since. And most amazing to me has been the way this Cup, when teaching about it, has impacted other pastors and missionaries and students around the world.

Through the years, as I've poured out my heart in messages and books, telling about this magnificent Cross, it was always the Father's Cup that captivated people. I've heard people say, over and over again, "Why didn't I know?" Some had been pastors or evangelists for over forty years, some held Ph.D. degrees, and some were young adults or teenagers looking for a purpose for which they could burn. Several of these youth are now preaching the gospel in the nations today.

## WHEN NATIONS RESPOND TO THE CUP

One night, while teaching about the Cup at an "Unquenchable Flame Conference" led by Pastor Greg Violi in Germany, people from all over Europe began running forward. This surprised me because I had not even given an altar call. I had been describing the Cup Jesus saw as He prayed in the garden, and when they began to see what was in that Cup, they realized they had completely ignored it for their whole Christian lives. All they could do was run forward, throw themselves on the floor, and repent. I still never gave an altar call, but nevertheless they came, repenting and crying out to God.

In a conference in Hong Kong the same thing happened. People literally screamed and ran forward. They wept on the floor, repenting and embracing the Cross and the Cup with sincere passion. The leader of this massive Asian network, Dr. Ernest Chan, who holds a Ph.D. from Fuller Theological Seminary, said, with trembling voice, "After forty years of ministry, I have never heard about the Cup!" He urged the people to look with all their hearts into the infinite depths of this Cup.

Most encouraging to me has been hearing what has happened when others looked into the Father's Cup and then began preaching it themselves, even in other nations.

Kathy, a missionary to Asian countries, said, "Dr. Sandy, I'm not the preacher in the family, my husband is. But when I read about the Father's Cup in your book, I knew I couldn't contain it. I preached it one day in Malaysia, and suddenly the people burst out weeping and wailing over what Jesus did for them. I had to wait almost an hour for the weeping to settle before I could go on."

Amazingly, the same thing happened when they traveled on to Borneo. But then she said something that completely took my breath away. "We have just received word that ISIS will be waiting for us in Bangladesh, the next place we are going. But I'm not afraid. When I think what Jesus did when He drank the Father's Cup, I only want to bring the Lamb the reward of His suffering!"

Her words broke me. Up to this point, I had found most American churches indifferent to this message about the Father's Cup. But now here was this missionary to Asia, whom I had never met, who had stumbled across my book on the Internet.[13] Her ministry had exploded with truth and fire when she spoke about the Father's Cup in dangerous countries. She was even willing to lay her life down for the Cross of Christ if necessary.

## HIS DISCIPLES STILL SLEEP

Look back now at Jesus in the garden. See him as He staggers over to His disciples, blood dripping from His hair, smearing His face, and splotching his robe. The grief in His heart so engulfs Him, that He feels He is about to die. "*My soul is deeply grieved to the point of death,*" He confides to them (Mark 14:34).

He asks them to stay awake and pray, but they cannot seem to grasp the gravity of His request. They are weighed down with their own sorrow, and while His anguished cries continue to ring out through the garden, they cannot hold their heads up. One by one, they nod back off to sleep. They simply don't understand the supreme magnitude of this prayer about the Father's Cup.

Yet we are no different. We live on the other side of the Cross, and still we have slept through Jesus' cries. We have overlooked the eternal significance of the Father's Cup. I know I had overlooked it. But when I looked with all my heart into the mind-numbing contents of this Cup, I was broken. I realized that I had wept more tears over the death of my dog, than over the death of my Lord.

You may be an evangelist who preaches all over the world or the pastor of a tiny church hidden in the mountains of Nicaragua. You may be a humble little mother in a remote village in Africa or India or South America, or you may be a Bishop over many churches in Europe or a mega church pastor in America. You may be a teenager looking for a purpose for which you could burn, or an elderly person who has loved God all your life but never heard of the Father's Cup.

Regardless of where you are in life, we all need to behold the Lamb and repent for neglecting the Cross. And most of all, for ignoring *the Father's Cup.*

Oh, please don't resist the stirring you feel in your spirit. This is the Holy Spirit drawing you. Don't be like the disciples in the garden, dozing through the cries of Jesus as He gazed into the Father's Cup?

If you feel the Holy Spirit convicting your heart, please join me in this prayer of repentance:

> *Dear Jesus, I don't even understand it all yet, but I want to tell You how sorry I am for only taking a casual glance at Calvary. Once a year at Easter, I have briefly glimpsed, but even then, it was with a sentimental, fleeting look, not with heart gripping focus and blood-earnest passion. I have cried more tears over my own wounds than over the wounds of my Lord. I have never wept in soul-shaking sorrow over the Cup You drank for me. For this I am deeply sorry.*
>
> *Forgive me, Lord, and open my eyes to a piercing revelation of the Lamb. Help me behold the Lamb of God. Holy Spirit, please remove the spiritual scales from the eyes of my heart and help me see, really see, for the very first time. With trembling heart, I draw near now to look into the depths of the Father's Cup.*

So let's look again inside that moon washed garden on the Mount of Olives where Jesus prayed. I have already given you a brief overview of the Father's Cup by telling you my story from the Methodist Sunday School class, but let's go deeper now.

Notice how all of nature seems stunned by Jesus' "loud crying and tears" (Hebrews 5:7). Why is He so horrified by this Cup? Do you know? When you see the contents of this Cup, I think you'll understand. It is more terrible than you can even imagine . . .

Two

# What is in this Cup?

## *Look Until You Can See*

All creation seems to hold her breath, listening to the heaving sobs of her Creator, as He prays. Doves cease their cooing. Insects silence their trilling and chirping. Jackals and wolves stop howling. All that can be heard is the gentle gurgle of the brook Kedron, running red and foaming with the blood of Passover lambs, funneling down from the temple mount.

Here on the dew-soaked ground of an olive orchard, the Lamb of God himself lies prostrate and bleeding, wrestling with God in prayer. Puritan theologian Thomas Goodwin said, "He was plunged head and ears in sorrow and had no breathing-hole."[14] Mark described him as "deeply distressed," using the word *ekthambeomai,* which means "horror-struck."[15]

Then suddenly, just across the ravine, the sound of shofars splits the night, and the gates of the temple fling open wide. Because it's Passover, the temple opens at midnight.[16] Joyous pilgrims, Jews from all over the world, throng into the courts to worship their God and to celebrate the feast of Passover. By tomorrow evening, each family will lift a lamb on a pole, roast it over the flames, and consume it together in the Paschal meal.

But over on the hill outside the city, He who is the fulfillment of the Passover Lamb, writhes in a bloody sweat. He knows that in only hours, just like the Pascal Lamb, He will be lifted on a pole and roasted over the flames of God's wrath.

Now His cries grow louder, rising in intensity, "Abba! Father! All things are possible for You; remove this CUP from Me." As His cry rises up to the heart of God, I can imagine the Father whispering to His Son:

> ***OH SON, MY BELOVED, DON'T YOU REMEMBER THE COVENANT WE MADE BEFORE THE CREATION OF THE WORLD? YOU AGREED TO DRINK MY CUP OF WRATH IN THE PLACE OF YOUR BRIDE. FOR THE JOY SET BEFORE YOU, YOU AGREED TO BECOME THE LAMB, SLAIN FROM THE FOUNDATION OF THE WORLD!***[17]

Now, as Jesus prays on His face in the garden, verses from the Old Testament swim through His mind.[18] He knows the Psalmist warns, *"In the hand of the Lord is a **cup** full of foaming wine mixed with spices"* (Ps 75:8). Ezekiel describes it as *"the **cup** of horror and desolation"* (23:33). Jeremiah tells about this Cup in His hand, *"filled with the wine of **my wrath**"* (25:15). Isaiah warns of *"the **cup** that made you stagger; from that **cup**, the goblet of **my wrath**"* (51:17, 22).

Jesus realizes full well that in this Cup is the eternal WRATH OF GOD against sin, and He knows that He must drink down every bitter drop of this punishment.[19] No wonder a view of this Cup is almost killing him as He says to His disciples, *"My soul is deeply grieved with sorrow to the point of death"* (Mark 14:35).

"Oh, Abba, is there any other way?" He cries. Then suddenly, blazing up in His mind, He sees Moses' burning bush, which, said Edwards, "represented the sufferings of Christ in the fire of God's wrath."[20] He knows that He is the fulfillment of that burning bush ablaze with holy fire (Exodus 3).

I can imagine him recalling how Abraham carried a cup or pail of fire in one hand and a dagger in the other as he lurched up the rocky slope of Mount Moriah. God had told him to sacrifice his son as a burnt offering, which meant he must slice him in pieces, cast him on the altar, and set him ablaze with the fire he carried (Gen 22:2).[21]

But Jesus also knows—He is the fulfillment of that burnt offering, for the Roman flagellum, with its shards of bone and nails and metal, knotted with a weight at the end of the leather strand, will shred Him like the lamb for the daily burnt offering. He will be cast down on the altar of the Cross and set ablaze as a burnt offering, which is actually known as the "holocaust offering." Yes, Jesus will become *God's Holocaust!*[22]

I'm sure He further sees himself as the fourth man in Nebuchadnezzar's fiery furnace, for He will be thrust into the incinerator of God's wrath, taking our punishment for sin. Edwards said, "He was brought to the mouth of the furnace that He might look into it, and stand and view its raging flames and see the glowing of its heat . . . . When He had a full sight of the wrath of God which He must suffer, the sight was over-whelming to Him."[23]

## "GOD TOOK MY HELL?"

Once again Jesus pushes up from His prone position and stumbles back to the disciples. He desperately needs their support in prayer, but still He finds them sleeping, dozing through the most crucial struggle of His life. And though His disciples won't get up and pray, God sends an angel from heaven to strengthen Him in this grueling battle.

Now, as He continues to pray, something even more horrifying strikes him. He recalls the verse in the Torah which says that *"anyone who is hung on a tree is under God's curse"* (Deut.21:23).

What is that curse? Bible scholar R. C. Sproul explains,

"Jesus became a curse for us, for He took the full punishment of hell during the Atonement."[24]

Can you believe it? Did you know Jesus took your hell when He drank the Father's Cup? That's why Isaiah wrote: *"the **punishment** that brought us peace was on him"* (Is 53:5, NIV). Charles Spurgeon said, "There was the cup, hell was in it, the Savior drank it." He will endure "the very pains of hell," said Jonathan Edwards.

Edwards explained that hell is actually "the outworking of the wrath of God," and the contents of the Father's Cup were "fully equivalent to the misery of the damned for it was the wrath of the same God."[25] Jesus himself called this His "baptism of fire" (Luke 12:50).

Arthur W. Pink said, "Not all the weeping and gnashing of teeth of the damned in the lake of fire" ever gave such a demonstration "of His infinite hatred of sin as did the wrath of God which flamed against His own Son on the cross."[26]

British theologian John R. W. Stott said, "We may even say that our sins sent Christ to hell," **not** in a battle down in hell after His body went into the grave, but **on the Cross** "before His body died."[27]

Now, more than ever, we can see why blood pressed out of his veins and streamed down on the ground. It was from a violent inner struggle as He grappled with the horrors of drinking the Father's Cup. Edwards said, He was "covered with clotted blood" which "had been forced through His pores through the violence of His agony."[28]

If you will look for one brief moment into the raging flames of wrath blazing in the Father's Cup, your doubts about hell will dissolve forever. Jesus saw that He would take our hell, in our place, but those who reject His offer of salvation, will drink *"the wine of God's fury which has been poured full strength into the cup of His wrath. He will be tormented with burning sulfur in the presence of the holy angels and the Lamb"* (Rev. 14:10, AMP).[29]

## THE CUP IN INDONESIA AND THE PHILIPPINES

When missionaries Mark and Cathy Kuntz began pastoring in the Philippines, they were amazed by how the people reacted to the Father's Cup. Cathy said, "When we first told them about the Cup in the garden, they almost seemed to freeze. They could hardly believe Jesus loved them so much He shed coagulated blood in Gethsemane. Then when we described the Cup of Wrath pouring down upon Jesus on the Cross, they ran to the altar sobbing out loudly." She continued, "We finally told them that they have become His reward, and this brought more crying and tears."

I've seen this happen with so many of our former students. Anton from Indonesia attended a nearby university, but when he heard about the "Revival of the Cross" happening at our camp, he felt compelled to come to one of our internships. He had only been saved two months, but God filled him with the fire of the Cross and soon he was back in Indonesia, preaching the power of the Father's Cup.

When he got back, he came out to our camp and told me with overflowing exuberance, "Dr. Sandy, I was preaching in a Bible College in Indonesia, and I asked the students, 'have you heard of the Father's Cup?' They said, 'No, tell us!'" He said, "I tried to tell them, but I couldn't even finish preaching. In the middle of my message, they just all began crying out. I didn't even try to give an altar call. They just cried out with all their hearts, repenting for not knowing or preaching about the Father's Cup!"

He told me another story about ministering to pastors in Bali. He said, "At first the pastors were a bit skeptical. Who was this young man who thought he had something to share with them? But Dr. Sandy, in the middle of my message about the Lamb and the Father's Cup, they burst out in loud crying and repenting for not preaching the complete gospel and for leaving out the Father's Cup!"

He then opened his iPad and showed me the video of them sobbing and shaking until it swelled into a crescendo of weeping pastors. Anton told me, "One pastor said, 'Now I truly understand that God took my hell!' I had to stop preaching because they were crying out, saying, 'Lord, forgive us, forgive us! From now on we will preach the Cross and the Father's Cup!'"

As you hear these stories, does it cause your heart to tremble? Oh, it does mine!

When I recall these stories and meditate on all that God has done, especially through these young men and women, it stirs my passion all over again. If you feel the same, please join me in this prayer:

> *Oh, Jesus, I want to embrace your Cross forever! Like Paul, I "resolve to know nothing . . . except Jesus Christ and Him crucified"* (1 Cor. 2:2). *For, when I look into the Cup which you drank for me, it breaks me. I see the hell, which I deserve for sin, boiling in this Cup. This is the Cup which I should drink myself, and my heart is completely undone when I think of it. Help me, Lord, to sense just one* ***tiny drop*** *of that Cup of wrath which You drank in my place. Help me to fellowship with You in Your sufferings. Help me to feel the depths of Your sacrifice, and may I never, never, ever forget what You have done for me!*

So even now, won't you find a quiet place to be alone with God? Begin meditating on the Cross and then focus your gaze on the contents of the Cup. See the wrath and hell burning and bubbling like a boiling lake of burning sulfur. Now see all that fiery wrath burning down on your sin. But see it blazing, not on you, but on *Jesus*. He is your substitute Lamb. Your sin is completely consumed in the Father's Cup of eternal wrath and judgment. And because of this incredible sacrifice, now you can be cleansed and purified to come into His holy presence forever. Oh, what a Savior!

Now that you have seen the ingredients in this Cup, you can see why He struggled so much, sweating blood and pleading with God to remove it. But there in the garden, He finally did surrender to its awful contents. How did He do it?

Of course, He wanted to do the will of His Father, but there was another reason. What was it? When you see it, you will understand what this cost Him. And most of all, you will see how much He really loves *you!*

Three

# Amazing Love

## *How Could Jesus Agree to Drink Your Cup?*

As Jesus grapples with God in prayer, clumps of warm, clotted blood still spill to the ground, pooling around His face. Jonathan Edwards said, "Those great drops of blood that fell down to the ground were a manifestation of an **ocean of love** in Christ's heart."[30]

This violent physical reaction is because Jesus faces the most difficult decision of His life. Will He surrender to the Father's Cup? Will He agree to drink down the blazing contents of God's wrath, enduring the horrors of hell? How could any man agree to plunge to such infinite depths of suffering?

If He agrees to drink the Cup, He will be bearing, not just one person's punishment, but the punishment for all humanity.

He will bear eternal wrath all condensed and thickened into one Cup. His suffering will be multiplied by billions!

Do you see what a monumental decision He faces? Edwards suggests that the Father asks Him, "What will you do? Is your love such that you will go on? Will you cast yourself into this dreadful furnace of wrath?"[31]

## WHAT DID HE SEE?

As the Father places this gruesome Cup before Him, Jesus knows He can say, "No Father, this is too much to ask! I have lived in the glory of Your presence through all eternity. I am innocent. Why should I be punished for sin I didn't commit? I cannot bear to endure the filth of sin, the punishment of Your wrath, and the separation from You it will bring!"

That would be perfectly understandable, yet if He refuses this Cup, the whole human race will plummet into hell.

But this is not what happens. He looks into that boiling Cup of wrath and He sees something compelling. It captures His heart. He would rather drink down every steaming drop of this Cup then let this precious treasure slip away.

What does He see? He looks into those raging flames of hell and He sees *you!* He knows you will be forever lost in eternal punishment if He doesn't stand in the gap and drink it in your place. But He cannot bear to live without *you!* His love for you far outweighs the horror of drinking the Cup.

Please let this sink in deep. The extent of His suffering reveals the magnitude of His love for *you*. As Charles Wesley wrote, "Amazing Love, how can it be that Thou my God would die for me!"[32] As Edwards wrote, "Christ's soul was overwhelmed with a deluge of grief, but this was from a deluge of love to sinners. His love is sufficient to overflow the world and overwhelm the highest mountains of its sins."[33]

## AVERTING WRATH FROM YOU AND ME

It's not that God is cruel and looking for people to punish. But God is holy, and He wants you near him. Sinful flesh cannot come into the presence of a holy God. So the Son of God races down to earth to throw himself in front of the explosion of God's wrath. The Bible calls this propitiation: *"In this is love, not that we loved God, but He loved us and gave His Son to be the* ***propitiation*** *for our sins"* (1 John 4:10).

*Propitiation?* What does that mean? It is not an intellectual word; it's biblical. It means, according to Professor Wayne Grudem in *Systematic Theology,* "A sacrifice to avert wrath and change it into favor."[34]

Think what this means to you. Read it in a personal way: "This is love, not that I loved God but that He loved me and gave His Son to take God's wrath on himself, averting it from me and turning it into God's gracious favor!"

It's like the true story of the father and daughter walking through the open-air market in Beirut, Lebanon. Suddenly an explosion went off as a suicide bomber blew himself up. In the chaos of the moment, the father looked around and saw another suicide bomber about to detonate his explosives. Without even thinking of himself, he left his child's side, raced toward the bomber, and tackled him to the ground. The bomb exploded, blowing up the young father, but saving countless lives, including his own daughter.[35]

In a far higher way, that is what Jesus did for you. He saw an explosion of God's wrath coming toward you. He saw the punishment of hell that would destroy you forever, if He didn't come. So, with love compelling Him, Jesus raced down to earth, flung himself in front of the impending detonation of wrath. Like the father in Beirut, He let that judgement explode on him, averting it from *you*. It happened when He drank the Father's Cup.

In all of heaven and earth, there is no more magnificent expression of love: *"Greater love has no one than this, that one lay down his life for his friends"* (John 15:13). That's why, only when you really look into the Cup Jesus drank for you, can you begin to comprehend *"the breadth and length and height and depth"* of the love of God for you (Eph. 3:18).

## CHINESE CHRISTIANS RESPOND TO THE CUP

One of the most precious demonstrations of the amazing love of God I've ever seen happened in a Bible College in downtown Hong Kong. For several days I poured out my heart about the Cross, which Chinese people love dearly. Though

Hong Kong had more freedom of religion than the mainland, many of these precious people would soon be persecuted for their faith. Perhaps that is why the Lord gave such a profound demonstration of His power to them.

When I began teaching about the Father's Cup, something amazing started happening all over the classroom. As these dear Christian people began looking into the flames of this Cup, several of them started falling out of their chairs to the floor, wailing and screaming up to God. I have only seen this a few times before, but I recalled reading how this would happen in Charles Finney's Revival meetings. People would fall off their chairs, hitting the floor and wailing in repentance.

Because I didn't understand their language, I had to ask what was happening. People began testifying in fast-speaking Mandarin, and finally my translator explained in English what they were saying. They said their hearts were being pierced when they looked into that Cup. Everyday this happened to more people and soon the room swelled with hungry visitors. They told of a tall angel who came into the room and pierced their hearts with a fiery spear. It happened when they looked into the Father's Cup and saw the full force of what Jesus did for them.

The crowd kept growing, and one day I looked up and saw a whole row of humble Chinese Christians from the underground church in the mainland. Lines of suffering marked their faces, but they were desperately hungry to hear more about the Cross. I watched these broken, humble people hungrily receive the message of the Father's Cup. Never have I felt such love for these people who have suffered so much for their faith.

Oh, I know this is what the world needs! Communist persecution against Chinese Christians has increased severely in the last ten years. And yet, many Chinese Christians have a vision to raise up 100,000 missionaries to go to every tribe and tongue and nation between the borders of China and Jerusalem. This is called the "Back to Jerusalem" movement.[36]

Because these precious people know how to suffer for Christ, God has called them to this tremendous mission to the Middle East. Many of them will indeed suffer, but they know that Jesus is worthy. He has already suffered for them, and they live to bring him the reward of His suffering.

## JESUS SURRENDERS

Look back now beneath the olive branches in the garden where Jesus lays prostrate in prayer. Tears burst from His eyes, mingling with the bloody sweat that coats His skin.

Finally, He rises to His knees and lifts His hands to heaven. In absolute surrender, he cries, *"Not My will, Father. But let Your will be done!"* Then He slumps back down to the ground, exhausted from blood loss and from wrestling with God in prayer.

Here on earth, we often read through this biblical account of Jesus praying in the garden, and our hearts remain unmoved. But if we could see beyond the clouds into the inner courts of heaven, I believe we would see a different story. This is the most monumental decision of all time. Our eternal destiny depended on it.

Long before the world's creation, the Son had agreed to become *"the Lamb slain from the foundation of the world."* Now, once again, He has agreed to drink the Father's Cup: *"For the joy set before Him,"* He has agreed to endure the Cross (Hebrews 12:2).

I can almost imagine the Father wiping away tears when he hears His Son's cry of relinquishment. Angels hold their breaths. All of heaven bows in hushed and holy awe.

And may we too bow our hearts in awe and reverence, as we leave the garden to climb the hill of Calvary. Draw near now to look up at Jesus, bleeding and hanging from two stakes of wood. Let's pray before we turn the page . . .

> *Father, my whole being trembles as I dare to climb that sacred hill outside Jerusalem. My heart stands still as I draw near to look reverently into this most colossal event of all time.*
>
> *I know this is the hinge of all human history. It is the summit of the Cross. It is the centrality of the whole Bible. It is the focus of the Father's gaze in heaven. With holy anticipation I come to behold the Lamb, punished in my place, as He drinks the Father's Cup . . .*

## Four

# Punished for Me!

### *The Substitute Lamb*

With bated breath, the Holy Spirit bids us now to climb the blood-stained hill of Calvary and stand on the crest of the mount. Experience the soft spring breeze blowing across your face. Feel the electricity filling the atmosphere. Sense the emotion crackling in the air. Hear the cries of grief and anger and pain all around you.

Lift your gaze to Jesus, the uncreated Creator of the Universe, suspended between heaven and earth. See thorns piercing His head, causing scarlet streams to pour down His cheeks, running into His ears and eyes and dripping into His beard. He is a visage of bruised and macerated flesh. He looks like He has been through a meat grinder.

Please don't cringe and look away from His blood. This is the blood that washes away your sin and opens the way to the holy of holies (Heb. 10:19). This is the blood that purifies your wedding garments (Rev. 7:9), and gives you power to overcome the enemy (Rev. 12:11). So focus your gaze upon His face, coated with crimson. Look deeply into those eyes. Let your own eyes lock with His. Can you see the love shining in His eyes? Let that ocean of love, which has compelled Him to Calvary, wash over you right now. Again, this is the greatest demonstration of love ever seen in heaven or earth.

## SIN DESCENDS ON THE SAVIOR

What is happening to Jesus now, as the sky blackens? It's as though God is covering the carnage of His own mangled Son with a cloak of protective darkness. "That darkness was a sacred concealment for the blessed person of our divine Lord," said Spurgeon.[37] And with this blanket of darkness, something grotesque falls upon the Son. God the Father takes all the sins of humanity and thrusts them down on Him. Like the priest in the temple, God lays His hands upon His Son and transfers our sins into Him.

Pause here and picture your grossest sin on Him. All the lust and pornography and sexual sin. All the bitterness and rage and murderous hatred. All the jealousy and gossip and gluttony. All the drug use and drinking and addictions. All the unbelief and doubt and fear. And don't forget all the pride and vain glory and selfish ambition, which hide beneath a veil of self-righteousness. Now see it all rolled down on Him. Like the scapegoat on Yom Kippur (Lev. 16), see the Lamb taking your sin on himself and carrying it into outer darkness.[38]

Look at Him now as He twists and thrashes under the terrible weight of sin. Indeed, He was *"pierced through for our transgressions, He was crushed for our iniquities"* (Is. 53:5). "God made Him who had no sin to be made sin for us" (2 Cor. 5:21), for He is *"the Lamb of God who takes away the sin of the world"* (John 1:29, KJV).

Come closer now, into the spiritual depths of this burning bush. See what God does about sin. See the furnace open as God prepares to cast His Son into its eternal blazing flames. We have seen how Jesus oozed blood as He wrestled in prayer at the mere thought of drinking the Father's Cup, but now He is about to *experience* it . . .

## THE CUP TIPS

As Jesus writhes under the heavy load of human sin, spikes tug against His hands. Ropes burn His arms, holding Him to the wood, preventing the spikes from tearing through the flesh of His hands. Raw wounds on His back scrape against the splintered wood. But suddenly, He stops thrashing. His body stiffens. His eyes fly open wide.

Look again into those eyes. His eyes tell the story. They are red from weeping and sleeplessness. They are bulging with tears, soaked with anguish, filled with unspeakable horror. See Him turn His gaze heavenward. His face pales. A look of shock and terror fills His eyes. He sees it coming. What is this? It is *the Father's Cup!*

Jesus braces himself against the oncoming tide, but He knows that as long as His Father is with Him, He can endure this appalling suffering. But wait . . . why is the Father turning His face away? Why is the Holy Spirit quietly taking flight? Why is God's presence lifting from the innocent Son of God?

What will Jesus do now? He is all alone. Why? Because sin must be punished, and none but Christ alone can bear this divine Judgment. Indeed, He alone is "the Lamb slain from the foundation of the world."

Can He still bear to go through with this? He could tear His hands loose or call thousands of angels to come and rescue Him. But no, though the presence of God withdraws, He relinquishes himself fully to the horrors of this Cup.

Behold now the innocent Lamb, as the ocean of God's wrath roars down upon Him. See wave after wave after wave of eternal punishment crashing over Him. See the Passover Lamb, skinned alive and lifted on a pole, roasting over the flames. See fire from heaven blazing down upon the burnt offering, causing Him to become the Holocaust Offering.

See this baptism of fire pour out upon Him as He endures the punishment of hell. Because *"all have sinned and fall short of the glory of God"* (Romans 3:23), we all should be punished for our sin. But right here on the Cross, Jesus is taking the punishment we deserve for sin—in our place!

Do you understand what this means? He came to drink the Father's Cup of wrath and hell in *your* place. He is *your* Substitute Lamb. He is *your* Scapegoat, bearing *your* sin into outer darkness.

But He is not carrying just one person's hell; this is the accumulated wrath for all humanity. This does not mean that all people are saved; it means they could be saved if they would turn to Christ. But to reject His offer of salvation, after He paid such an infinite price, is to miss the glorious opportunity to be born again and to live with Him forever.

And yet, do people today really know what He did for them? Do they even care? This true story illustrates why we must let people know the magnitude of what He did for them at Calvary.

One day in a Catholic church, a Cardinal told the story of three young men who decided to play a trick on the priest in the church. Each one would make up grotesque stories of sin to confess to the priest. The first two boys told their stories and went away giggling. The third young man stepped forward and began confessing his sin. By now the priest discerned what they were doing, so he called for an act of penance from the third boy. Pointing to the crucifix in the corner of the room, he told the boy to go kneel at the foot of the Cross and look up at Jesus. "Now tell Him three times—'All this you did for me, and I don't give a *damn!*'"

The boy knelt and spoke the mocking words, twice with contempt. Then, as he started to speak it a third time, something came over him. Suddenly, he saw the suffering of Jesus and conviction gripped him. He tried to say, "All this you did for me, and . . . I don't . . . give . . . " He fell over sobbing, overwhelmed with conviction. In this state of repentance, he prayed to give his life to Jesus Christ, and he was never the same. "I know this is true," said the Cardinal who was telling the story. "I was that young man!"[39]

Do you see? Just like those young men, though people have a vague understanding of what Jesus did for them, they really don't give a ___________. If they did, they would fall on their faces in repentance like the third young man in the story.

What then is the answer? We must tell them what Jesus did for them, especially about the Father's Cup of eternal punishment. If the true Church would climb the hill of Calvary and gaze into the Father's Cup of Wrath and Hell, something profound would happen. Our hearts would blaze and tremble with the holy passion of God, and He would give us the power of the Holy Spirit to proclaim the complete gospel of Jesus Christ!

Yes, it is time for the Cup to be revealed so our hearts can be filled with true passion for the Lamb!

## THE CUP IN KENYA

I want to tell you now about the first time I took a team of young adults to Kenya to help in a pastor's conference. At first the pastors resisted the teaching (because I was a woman). But when they heard about the Father's Cup, everything changed. They said, "We have always preached prosperity and demonology, but the power of the Cross and the Cup will set Kenya ablaze!"

After the conference, Pastor John came up and laid his head on my shoulder, trembling and weeping. "For the rest of my life I will preach this message of the Cross and the Cup!" he promised me. As a boy, John's father had forced his hand into a fire, causing excruciating pain. "I am not your real father," he sneered, chasing him out of the house. Today John Denge has one of the top worship CDs in all of Kenya, and his radio program reaches the entire nation. "This is the message that must be preached," he sobbed, "and I will preach it through all of Kenya!"[40]

One day in Kenya, we took a busload of children from Pastor Newton's orphanage, "The Gideon's Soldiers," and brought the message of the Cross into the nearby village. Draping several sheets sewn together over a bus, we showed "The Passion of the Christ" movie. I watched the people's faces as they saw cruel Romans ripping Jesus' flesh to bits with the scourge. The people had barely even heard of Jesus, but when they saw the God who came to earth in human flesh and laid down His life on a Cross, they wept and wept.

After the scourging scene, we stopped the movie, and Pastor Allan rose to the platform, thundering out a gospel message in Swahili. He told about the Cup of punishment that Jesus Christ drank for them, in their place. "He was punished for you! He took your hell!" he cried with all his heart.

"Punished for me?" they cried. Their powers of Voodoo and witchcraft and Islam never had a god who was punished for their sin. This was the one true God who loved them so much that He stood in their place and took their hell. When Sophie and Pastors Allan and Newton gave the altar call, half the people rushed to the front, crying out to be saved.[41]

I stood back, tears streaming down my face as I saw the power of the true gospel exploding in an African village. Rarely will a Western evangelist go into these hidden little villages where no one would ever see what they did, but God saw it. And I'm sure He was pleased, for nothing is so dear to His heart as seeing His Son, the Lamb who was slain, receive the reward of His suffering.

You will find that, as you include this message of the Cross and the Father's Cup in your gospel message, your own heart will burn, and you will know you are bringing Jesus the reward He deserves. If that is what you want, pray sincerely:

> *Dear Jesus, I promise you that for the rest of my life I will teach and preach and tell of the Father's Cup. Never again will I preach a watered-down, Cup-drained gospel. Grant me to be a voice like*

*John the Baptist, crying in the wilderness of this world, "Behold the Lamb of God who takes away the sin of the world!" With all my heart I will live to bring Jesus, the Lamb who was slain, the reward of His suffering for surrendering to the Cross and drinking the Father's Cup.*

Come now to hear the most horrific cry ever heard in heaven or earth. This is what scholars call "the cry of dereliction." See what this cry, from the lips of Jesus Christ, did to the heart of the Father . . .

Five

# The Cry of the Ages

## *Piercing the Heart of the Father*

Jesus drinks and drinks and drinks, swallowing down every scalding drop of the Father's Cup. For three grueling hours He has been engulfing this burning substance, but finally, He can take no more.

He throws back His head. His eyes fly open wide. Hot tears burn in His eyes. Terror fills them. Now they roll upward as though looking for something . . . for Someone. Desperately He searches for His Father, but He is nowhere to be found.

Suddenly, He thrusts himself down on the spike in His feet to fill His lungs with air. The wounds tear open again. Fresh streams of blood spill down His feet and toes, dripping down the vertical beam and pooling on the ground.

His mouth moves as though He wants to speak. The crowd hushes. In the first three hours He spoke three times, once to forgive His murderers, next to save a sinner beside him, and then to care for His mother. But now, for almost three hours, He remains silent. Do you know why? Because He has been drinking His Father's Cup. The torment is too deep for words.

Please notice He never complains about the mocking and spitting, the pummeling, the scourging, or the spiking of hands and feet, but now He can restrain himself no longer. The agony mounts within Him like hot molten lava, rising within the volcano of His heart until finally it is ready to erupt. The volcanic emission blasts from His lips in a torrent of absolute anguish. In a guttural, animal-like roar He cries:

***ELOI, ELOI, LAMA SABACHTHANI? MY GOD, MY GOD, WHY HAVE YOU FORSAKEN ME?"*** (Mark 15:34).[42]

The crowd stands stunned. All of nature seems to hold its breath. The wind stops blowing, birds scatter, dark clouds cease churning, the sun still hides its face. Creation's uncreated Creator on a Cross releases the saddest, most poignant, most earth-shaking words ever spoken on this planet.

Yes, never in heaven or earth has such a cry been uttered. Most unthinkable of all, God the Son discharges this terrifying cry up in the face of His Father. God screams at God.

## THE FATHER'S HEART

As this cry blazes from the lips of the Son, it is as though a red-hot rock of lava, dripping with grief and pain, heaves from the lips of the Lord. It hurls up through the clouds, flinging into the courts of heaven, searing with a heavy thud into the heart of God.

Notice that His Son doesn't cry, "Why have You poured your wrath and punishment upon Me?" "Why have you unleashed Your judgment upon Me?" "Why have You plunged Me into the utter depths of hell?" No, He knew all this would happen. God had shown it to Him before the creation of the world, and then He showed Him again in the garden.

But the cry that tears from His lips is "*Why have You FORSAKEN Me?* Why have You *deserted* Me? Why have You *abandoned* Me in my time of greatest need? Why have You left Me all alone in the midst of this unspeakable torture? Father, I could endure this horrible punishment for sin if I had your presence sustaining Me, but why have You lifted your presence from Me while I drink Your Cup?"

Can you imagine how this made the Father feel? I can almost see the Father, gripping His chest and doubling over in heartache. These devastating words break Him to His knees, for when His Son suffers, He suffers even more.

Have you ever had to see your child suffer and there was nothing you could do? I know how I felt when I had to watch my own son endure a debilitating injury which robbed him of his career and still causes endless sleepless nights. Everything in me wants to run to his side and ease his pain.

It's like that beautiful true story of the father of Derek Redmond at the Barcelona Olympics. When Derek's hamstring suddenly snapped and he fell rolling in pain to the track, an old man was seen rising up from the stands and elbowing his way through the crowd. Derek twisted in pain on the racetrack, but finally, he pushed himself to his feet and began dragging himself toward the finish line. The old man was Derek's father, who felt the pain and anguish of his own son. He knew he had to somehow help him.

The father stumbled down from the bleachers, reaching the track field. He broke through the line of officials who tried to stop him and rushed out on the track to the side of his son. Throwing his arm around his boy, together they hobbled their way toward the finish line. Not a dry eye could be found in the stadium.

In a far higher way, the Father looks down from the grandstand of heaven, His own heart throbbing with grief. How the Father must have yearned to leave His throne and rush to the side of His Son. His Son had just screamed up in His face, and everything in Him longed to run to Him and ease His suffering. He ached to help Him through the terrors of drinking this torturous Cup, but He didn't. Do you know why?

Because of sin! Because Jesus was imbued with our sin, the ineffably pure and holy God had to remove His presence from Him. This is why the Son must bear this agony alone.

Our sin caused this abandonment by God. Can you believe it? Our sin caused His Son to be punished. Our sin caused God to forsake God.

Oh, may we hate the sin that caused our Savior such excruciating agony! And may we never join the culture of our day which denies the reality of sin! This is what sin did to our Savior![43]

I tell you when I try to wrap my thoughts around it, my heart is completely undone. Can you see how this earth-shaking cry, throws open a window into the agony of the Father's Cup? It gives us a terrifying glimpse into the magnitude of Jesus' suffering when the waves of divine wrath smashed down upon Him.

This is indeed the purpose for which He came as He is *"smitten by God and afflicted;"* He is *"pierced . . . chastened . . . crushed"* by the very hand of God (Is. 53:4, 5, 8, 10). Spurgeon said, "He drained that Cup of hell until there is not a dregs left for any of His people."[44]

Oh, can you see that this is what has been missing from our gospel! We've been preaching a Cup-drained, hell-drained, blood-drained gospel, and it is *incomplete!* But this message of the Cup will set your theology ablaze. It will drive out deception in the Church. It will cause your preaching to burn and your whole life to be ignited with the fire of the Cross, and this time it will be a fire that never burns out. Ultimately it will have the potential to spark a Revival that sets your nation ablaze with holy fire!

## AFRICAN PASTORS

African Pastor Henry told me, "Preachers today want to get rich from their people so they preach a message of prosperity. You know how it goes— 'plant your seed into my ministry and God will bless you!' But," he said with firm resolve, "that's manipulation and it's wrong!" He continued, "The message that will change lives and change this land is the message of the Cross and the Father's Cup. This message has fire, and it will spread Revival through Kenya and all of Africa!"

Pastor Zachy said that when he first heard this message of the Father's Cup, it pierced his heart. But what cut him even more was when he looked around his country and saw how the message of the Cross and the Father's Cup were missing from the pulpits in the Church in Africa. He began sharing this message everywhere he could, because he said, "This is the message that carries *fire!*"

Back in America, during Covid 19, I decided to video many of my classes, teaching about the Father's Cup and other subjects related to the gospel. We put the videos into a Bible School format and simply named it The School of the Cross. When the African pastors saw it mentioned on Facebook, they jumped on board and asked if they could join the school. I said, "No, you won't *join* the school; you will *teach* it!" They were young, strong, intelligent young men and a few women, and I believed they could do a wonderful job. I provided books and exams and a Certificate and invited Pastor Zachy to be president of the school. The school took off and within two years we had thirteen Schools of the Cross in Kenya and Uganda.

Pastor Zachy said, "When I began teaching and preaching this message, God started spreading a fire. It became an Awakening because the fire of God awakens people. They began to feel stirred to teach and preach and minister for Jesus. It's an Awakening that keeps on spreading.

This email from Pastor Edmond in Kenya says it all:

> Sunday morning, I was sharing on Jesus on the Cross. When I described how He was howling like a wounded animal as the fires of God's wrath were being poured on Him, the church was captivated, and you could hear the sobs. Then when I cried the cry of dereliction, wow, the church busted out with cries all over. I had to give them time to weep as they beheld He whom they had pierced . . . . The room was charged with God's glory! Doc, it was awesome! Many lives were restored. The whole church ran to the altar without being called and they wept before the Lamb of God. May the Lamb that was slain, receive the reward of His suffering!
>
> Blessings, Pastor Edmond

My heart stood still when I read what happened in that little African church, for I know this is what we need. This is what we must have! We need Revival, but it must be anchored into the solid rock foundation of the pure gospel. If not, it will burn brightly for a while but eventually fizzle out like smoke in the wind. This is why the full, true, and complete gospel message must remain at the heart of Revival.

The story, however, is not yet finished. Come now to see how this horrific howl that wrenches from Jesus' lips shook the earth. Come see what happens to the rocks, to the veil in the temple, and most of all, to the hearts of those who love Him . . .

Six

# Pierced

## *Carving a Love Wound into the Heart*

The blood-curdling cry from the Savior of the world still hangs in the air. People stand in shock, some smirking, some grieving, some jolted by such a horrific howl.

Look down at the little woman standing near the Cross. There she stands, Jesus' own mother, weeping shamelessly in the arms of the young disciple. She grips her chest as pain claws her heart.

As a mother, I can almost feel her heartache. I see her breaking from John's grasp and rushing to the feet of her Son. I hear her sobbing, "Jesus, I won't forsake You! I'm here for You!"

She doubles over in pain, falling to the ground, weeping wildly. Then suddenly the words of the old prophet flash before her. Long ago in the temple, Simeon had told her, *"and a sword will pierce even your own soul—to the end that thoughts from many hearts may be revealed"* (Luke 2:35). Now, as she slumps at the feet of her Son, she can feel the blade of the sword cutting raggedly through her soul.

Suddenly, Mary hears Jesus groan, *"I am thirsty!"* (John 19:28). She looks around and spots soldiers gambling and guzzling posca, a cheap vinegar wine.

One of them, hearing Jesus' cry, stabs a stalk of hyssop into a sponge, dips it in posca, then lifts it up to Jesus. The vinegar stings His cracked lips, but it wets His tongue so He can speak His final words.

Now, with His mouth moistened, Jesus pushes down hard on the spike in His feet to lift His lungs for air. He prepares to shout His final words, for He knows that at last His work on earth is done.

Though it looks like defeat, in reality a colossal triumph has taken place. With all His might, Jesus bellows, *"IT IS FINISHED!"* (John 19:30). Do you know what this means? Above all else, this shout of victory means that Jesus has drunk to the dregs the final drops of *the Father's Cup.*

Yes, because sin has been fully punished, the devil has no more sin to feed on. Satan and all his principalities and powers have been exposed and overcome on the Cross: *"And having disarmed the powers and authorities, he made a public spectacle of them, triumphing over them by the cross"* (Col. 2:13, NIV).

Though Satan has bruised His heel, as promised by God long ago, the Seed of the Woman has crushed the serpent's head (see Gen. 3:15). Now, even as God finished His work of creation on the sixth day, the Lord finishes His work of redemption with His sixth word from the Cross.[45]

And now, with one final burst, Jesus cries, "*FATHER, INTO YOUR HANDS I COMMIT MY SPIRIT*" (Luke 23:46).[46] Even as God rested from His work of creation on the seventh day, Jesus rests from His work of redemption with His seventh word. And now it happens . . . Jesus' heart ruptures!

## THE DIVINE RUPTURE

Thunder booms and lightning lashes the sky. The earth groans and the ground begins to shake. It suddenly seems that the whole universe responds to this final cry from the Lord. Lightning flashes like bright shining floodlights. Thunder crashes like loud clashing cymbals. The wind whistles like blaring trumpets. The ground rumbles like the sound of deep rolling bass drums.

It's as though Almighty God blazes through eternity: "*Behold the Lamb of God, who takes away the sin of the world!*" And then, over in the temple, to the shock of attending priests, the heavy veil tears in two from top to bottom. Only the hand of God could have torn this massive veil, which took three hundred priests to handle it.

Do you know what this means? Scripture explains: "*Therefore, brethren since we have confidence to enter the holy place by the blood of Jesus, by a new and living way which He inaugurated for us through the veil, that is, His flesh . . . . Let us draw near with a sincere heart"* (Heb. 10:19-20).

But the reason we can now draw near is not simply because of the tearing of a veil in the temple, but because of what this veil signifies. It represents, as the verse above says—*"the veil, that is, **His flesh**."* Yes, Jesus' flesh is the true veil. Now His own human heart has ruptured like a ripped veil, torn apart to open the way back to God.[47]

Oh, what a Savior! What a massive plan of salvation! What an immeasurable sacrifice! Not just on His part, but on the part of His own Father! Do you see why, above all, the Lamb is worthy to receive the reward of His suffering?

Now the earth quakes, women scream in fear, and men beat their breasts in remorse. A soldier strides up with a heavy sledgehammer. He lifts it over his head, preparing to smash it down on Jesus' knees so that He cannot breathe. He doesn't know that Jesus has already released His spirit to the Father.

Suddenly, the skies explode with thunder and lightning. Trees on the hillside thrash and flashes of lightning spear the ground at Calvary. The earth shakes violently, and the soldier drops His heavy mallet. It's as though God himself is shouting— "Don't you dare break a bone of My Passover Lamb!" (See Exodus 12:46).

Another soldier draws back His spear and plunges it deep into Jesus' side. The tip of the blade drives all the way up to the pericardium, the lining around the heart. John wrote, *"one of the soldiers pierced His side with a spear, and immediately blood and water came out"* (John 19:34).[48]

Yes, even as Moses struck the rock in the wilderness, causing rivers to flow from the rock, now the Rock of Ages himself has been struck, causing rivers to flow from His wounded side. And even as the streams in the wilderness quenched the thirst of millions, the river that flows from the heart of the Lamb will quench the thirst of billions.

## THE LOVE WOUND[49]

I can still see the little mother, Mary, standing there with John. They huddle so near the Cross they can feel the warm spray of blood and water showering out on their faces and throats and hands. John holds Mary closely as she weeps out her grief, and the sword continues to pierce to the depths of her soul.[50]

Yes, a sword pierced Mary's soul as she looked up at her Son, bleeding like a Lamb on the Cross. But she is a picture of the Church, whose heart will be pierced as she beholds the bleeding Lamb of God.

Oh Beloved, please let the Cross do its soul-piercing work in your own heart as well. Don't let this opportunity pass you by. Don't let the Cup go to waste. Don't squander one drop of this boiling Cup. Let it burn deep. It will ignite a passion within you that will never stop trembling.

Spurgeon said, "The piercing of the heart begins when we look upon the pierced one."[51] Even as the veil in the temple was torn, the veil must be torn from our own hearts too, for we are the temple of the Holy Spirit. Just like Mary, as we behold the Lamb, the sword will begin to pierce us deep within. It will rend our hearts as the prophet Joel said, *"Rend your heart and not your garments"* (2:13).

In his book, *The Secret of Smith Wigglesworth's Power,* Peter Madden said, "The reality and extent of revival depend on the depth of the incision of the Cross of Christ in the heart."[52] For it is out of this piercing that rivers of love, rivers of healing, rivers of revival, and rivers of life will stream.

A. B. Simpson, founder of the Christian and Missionary Alliance movement said, "We may not preach a crucified Savior without also being crucified men and women . . . . The cross that Paul speaks about was burned into his very flesh, was branded into his being, and only the Holy Spirit can burn the true cross into our innermost being."[53]

This is why our own hearts need to be pierced like Mary's,[54] for the world won't fully receive the message of our crucified Christ until they see it issuing through the heart of a crucified Bride.[55]

## HE STILL PIERCES HEARTS

At Pentecost, when Peter preached the gospel through burning lips of fire, the people were *"PIERCED to their hearts"* (Acts

2:37). Through the years, I've discovered that the Cross still pierces hungry hearts.

Our team ministered in an amazing Latino church in London. After teaching on the Father's Cup, we invited the people to come forward who wanted to embrace the Cross more deeply. We began praying for God to pierce their hearts with the power of the Cross.

Pastor Marcos reached out for prayer, but before anyone could even touch him, the lightning of God struck him down. He fell back over the steps of the altar and gripped his chest. He groaned with loud wailing as God himself was piercing his heart. Later he told me, "I could feel something inside me shifting. I know I will never be the same!"

This is what we must have! We need a sovereign piercing from the hand of the Lord. In the garden of Eden, a flaming sword guarded the way into God's presence. Now He pierces our hearts with the flaming sword of the Cross and it opens the way into more of God's presence.

My ministry assistant, Mary, and I saw this sacred wounding one morning in a little church in Wath, England. I was preaching about the Lamb of God in Pastor Peter Morris's church. He was weeping on the front row, his face red as he took the message of the Father's Cup deeply into his heart.

But suddenly, his son, Nathan, sitting behind him, who had only been saved for a month, gripped his chest and began groaning. I stopped teaching and gently laid my hand on his chest, simply co-operating with what God was already doing.

Nathan fell weeping from his chair and went home and wept all day over the Cross.

Over the next few years Nathan pressed into God with all of his heart. His hunger for the Cross intensified, and he began preaching the gospel all over England and in crusades around the world. The Lord started moving in his meetings with powerful miracles, and he always pointed to the blood of the Cross as the source of God's healing power.

One night Nathan had come over to America to preach in an "Open Heavens Conference" in my own Church of His Presence in Daphne, Alabama with Pastor John Kilpatrick. Nathan started to preach, but suddenly the Holy Spirit arrested him. He couldn't get the words out. The power of God swept down over him and melted him to the floor. Pastor Kilpatrick got up and said, "This reminds me of Father's Day 1995!"[56]

This was the beginning of the Bay of the Holy Spirit Revival which burned on for several years. With my own eyes I saw the hundreds of amazing miracles taking place in the revival. And though thousands of miracles took place as Nathan and Pastor Kilpatrick took the revival around the nation, always Nathan boldly proclaimed, "This revival is not about miracles. It's about the Cross and the blood of the Lamb!"

## CRUCIFYING IMPURE MOTIVES

You may aspire to have a great ministry yourself, but oh, please hear me! I'm not talking about another cool experience with

God so that you can have a powerful ministry. God's fire is costly. It cost Him everything, and it cannot ever be used for our personal glory. That's why this heart wound is so needed. It cuts away impure motives, humbles our pride, crushes our selfish ambition, and severs our need to be seen. It fills us with one burning passion—to live to bring Jesus the reward He deserves for drinking the Father's Cup.

One Sunday afternoon, I watched Youth with a Mission's Bible teacher Joy Dawson on You Tube. The program on P.T.L. must have been from forty years ago, but her words spoke to me with a cutting blade of conviction that brought me to my knees. Joy was telling her story of being convicted by God of her own sin of self-glory. She said, "Only God knows what's in our hearts," but then she began telling about the time the Lord had shown her pride in her heart three separate times in one week.

Oh, I tell you her words severed my heart with a veritable spear of conviction. She told how the Lord had broken her heart over her sin of pride and vain glory. She was so vulnerable and open, and it opened me wide to search my own heart. I felt the pain of the same sin in my life, and I couldn't bear it. I fell to the floor and repented with godly sorrow for my sin. I don't know how long it lasted, but when I stood up, I knew something deep and ugly had been uprooted from my soul.

If this is what you long for, bow before the Lord and look into this Cup until something happens to you. Until you can *"fellowship in the sharing of His sufferings"* (Phil. 3:10).

Look deeply until, with the eyes of your heart, you can see your impure motives crushing down upon Jesus in waves of utter darkness. Now see that Cup tip . . . Watch the flames bursting out of the Cup and roaring down on Him.

Keep on looking until you can almost hear that earsplitting cry, *"My God, My God, why have You forsaken Me?"* Hear God scream up at God. Let this horrific heart cry of Jesus pierce into your heart until you are utterly wrecked, shaken to the core, undone forever by a revelation of the Father's Cup.

It will break you. It will melt you at His feet. It will pierce to the depths of your soul. It will cut away all the false motives and vain glory, hiding beneath the surface. It will change everything. If this is what you want, cry out now to God:

> *O God, I open my heart to You. Please take the sword of your Cross and cut to the core of my soul. Drive the blade in deep and slice out everything that doesn't glorify You. Let the point penetrate to the quick of my being. All I want is You, so please cut away every fleshly desire. Ignite a passion for the Cross within me until my heart bleeds only for You.*[57]

If you believe that God is touching you, reach up and help Him drive the Cross into your soul. Receive it. Draw it in deeply. Let the bittersweet blade cut to the quick of your deepest desire for self-glory. Let all other motives fall away except one. Let your highest purpose, your most fervent passion, your one compelling motive be to bring Jesus the reward of His suffering for drinking the Father's Cup.

*Dear Jesus, cut away the scales from my eyes and let me see Your blazing Cup. Let me gaze upon the flames until my heart is fully consumed. Let me taste, if possible, one drop of that holy fire. Let consuming passion flow from me. Then through my own pierced heart, let me bring to my people and to my nation a Revelation of the Father's Cup.*

Let's go now to that glorious morning when the Holy Spirit raised Jesus from the dead. Discover why this Resurrection Power of God is vital for you, to lead you in your Christian life.

Then, as we look at the influence of this power in the nations, see what happened when a little Jewish lady, walking down the street in Peru, heard the full gospel preached from an open door to the street. Read also the story of the chief of police in a large city in India, where our team was holding a pastor's conference. If I dared say anything about the false gods in India, I could be handcuffed and thrown in jail. Problem was, no one told me this was against the law. Guess what I said? And guess what happened . . . ?

## Seven

# Resurrection Power

### *The Power Outflowing from His Resurrection*

Quietly and without notice, a gentle wind blows into the garden where Jesus is buried. The breeze flows through the garden, stirring spring flowers and fanning early budding fruit trees. Leaves rustle and shine. The wind heads straight for the stone which blocks the opening to the tomb.

He whiffs right through the stone, for this is not a wind at all. He is the precious Holy Spirit, the third Person of the Triune Godhead. Even as the Spirit of God "hovered trembling" over the body of waters at creation (see Genesis 1:2),[58] He now "hovers, trembling" over the body of Jesus. All of heaven must be watching as the Father, accompanied by hundreds of thousands of angels, looks down from the balcony above.

As the Holy Spirit lingers above the corpse of Jesus, He looks at Him with longing. Being the most tender and sensitive one in the Godhead, it would have grieved Him profoundly when He withdrew His presence from Jesus on the Cross.[59] He yearns desperately to fill Him and clothe Him again.

As the Father looks down, I'm sure His heart must surge with joy over what is about to happen. He has suffered unthinkable pain as He watched the scourge, the thorns, the spikes, and the filthy sludge of human sin bear down upon His Son. But the climax of agony came when He tumbled His Cup of Wrath and punishment upon His Beloved.

## THE RISEN LAMB

With His heart bursting with love and elation, the Father finally shouts:

***"NOW, HOLY SPIRIT, RAISE MY SON FROM THE DEAD!"***

Exhaling softly, the Spirit of God breathes into the spirit, the soul, and the body of Jesus. Suddenly, His heart starts to beat. He takes a breath. His whole body quickens. Life from God fills His entire being.

His eyes flutter and slowly open. He sits up straight and rises out of His grave clothes. They sink in like the suction of a vacuum. As He stands, angels fall backward. His glory floods the tomb, for He is "*the sole expression of the glory of God [the Light-being, the out-raying or radiance of the divine]*" (Hebrews 1:3, AMP). Yes, now the light of eternity shines out, for "*the Sun of Righteousness*" rises "*with healing in His wings and His beams*" (Malachi 4:2, AMP).

Tradition holds that over in the temple the light on the candelabra blows out, for the "*light of the world*" has risen from the tomb. And even as the priest waves the first fruit sheaves of barley, celebrating the Feast of First Fruits, Jesus Christ, the first fruits from the dead, steps out upon the earth.

That evening, as His disciples hover behind closed doors, Jesus walks right through the walls. "Shalom!" He greets them. His smile drenches each one with the presence of God. Holding out His hands, He shows them His wounds. Every wound bleeds glory. Indeed, "*His brightness was like the sunlight: rays streamed from His hand, and there [in the sunlike splendor] was the hiding place of His power*" (Habakkuk 3:4, AMP).

Tenderly, He breathes out upon them all, saying, "*Receive the Holy Spirit*" (John 20:20). The disciples inhale, breathing in His glory. His eyes sparkle as He commissions them, "*Go into all the world and preach the* ***gospel*** *to all creation*" (Mark 16:15). Now the disciples go out preaching the gospel of Jesus Christ in "the power outflowing from His resurrection" (Phil. 3:10, AMP).

## "THEY'VE TAKEN AWAY MY LORD"

Today, however, it seems we preach everything *but* the gospel. And even if we do preach it, we usually forget to tell about the most vital aspect of the Cross—the Father's Cup!

When Mary Magdalene came to the tomb of Jesus on that Resurrection morning, she found His body missing. She rushed to the disciples and cried, "They have taken away the Lord out of the tomb, and we don't know where they have laid Him!" (John 20:2).

That's how I feel when I look around and see how seldom the true gospel is preached today. Rarely to we hear the Cross or the Father's Cup mentioned. Like Mary Magdalene, I feel like "They have taken away my Lord and I don't know where they have laid Him!"

It reminds me of the young mother who parked her car to run in and pick up some food for her baby, leaving the baby asleep in the car. But while in the store, she momentarily forgot the baby and picked up a few more items. Then she rushed back out to the car, only to find that thieves had broken into the car and stolen her baby.

That's what has happened in the Church. Thieves have broken in and stolen the Baby! They preach what they call the "gospel," but they have lost the pure essence of the true gospel. While we've busily carried on our activities, the central message of *"Christ and him crucified"* has gone missing. The Cross and the Father's Cup have essentially been forgotten.

"They have taken away my Lord, and I don't know where they have laid Him!"

Do you see why we must tell the whole gospel? If we fail to explain the Cup, which Jesus drank as our Substitute Lamb, we are gutting the central truth of the message. Spurgeon said it best: "If you put away the doctrine of the substitutionary sacrifice of Christ, you have **disemboweled** the gospel and torn from it its very heart."[60]

Again, Jonathan Edwards' said that the primary reason, "the principal errand," the paramount purpose Jesus came to accomplish on earth was to drink the Father's Cup.[61] So once more I ask—if this be true, then why do we hear so little about it today?

Through the years, I've had hundreds of Christians say, "Why didn't anyone ever tell me about the Father's Cup?" I've grappled with this question for years. I'm sure one reason is because some preachers fear discussing God's wrath. Yet we can never fully understand God's love if we don't understand the wrath He endured for us. I've also discovered that another reason we haven't heard more about the Father's Cup is because of a huge language barrier.

Evangelical Scholars use terms like "Divine Justice Satisfied," or "Appeasement of God's wrath," or "Penal Substitution," or "Propitiating Divine Wrath." These terms are excellent theology, but they zip right over most people's heads. Very few preachers want to turn off their listeners by using such intellectual terms. So, as I said to one of my professors at Fuller Theological

Seminary, "Sir let's change the language, but not the truth! Let's use the language Jesus used. Jesus simply called it *the Father's Cup*."

Jesus never called it "Justice Satisfied" or "Penal Substitution." He used down-to-earth language. In Matthew, Mark, and Luke He called it "**the CUP**." In John, He settled it by telling Peter, ***"The CUP which the Father*** *has given Me, shall I not drink it?"* (John 18:11). That's why I keep insisting—Jesus called it *the Father's Cup!*

## IT'S TIME TO REVEAL THE CUP

In the beginning of this book, I asked, "Do You Tremble?" When Jesus looked into the Cup as he prayed in the garden, He trembled so violently that blood squeezed out of His vessels, oozed out of the pores of His skin, and dripped in large clots to the ground! Do you see why I say—**it is time for the church to TREMBLE as well!**

Yes, the time at last has come for the Cup our Lord prayed about in the garden to come out of the shadows. It's time for the Church to grasp once again the fullness of what God did for us on the Cross. It's time to be revived with Truth. It's time for the spirit of Revival to sweep down upon the Church, like on the day of Pentecost when flecks of fire burned down and the wind of the Spirit blew this fire all over the world.

Not only will looking into this fiery Cup start a revolution in your own heart, ultimately, it will lead to a Reformation in the Church. Martin Luther led the great Protestant Reformation. He brought the Church out of the dark ages of religious blindness by bringing back the gospel. Nailing his 95 Theses to the church door in Wittenberg, Germany, he called for a recovery of the "true gospel."[62]

The time has come once again for the "true gospel" to be restored to the Church. It will cause a seismic shift, a veritable earthquake in the body of Christ. The Church will tremble and everything that can be shaken will topple and fall away. Once again, the Crucifixion and Resurrection of Jesus Christ will be central.

Indeed, it is time for a Revival that never smolders or smokes out because it keeps the Cross in the center. It's time for Revivals to be anchored in the Cross and the Cup, for this is where the eternal flame burns on and on forever.

## WHERE WAS THE VICTORY WON?

Through the years, I've heard people say, "It's time to move beyond the Cross on to the power of the Resurrection." Others have said, "The crucifixion is the place of defeat, the resurrection is the place of victory." This is serious error.

John R. W. Stott explains, "We are not to regard the cross as defeat and the resurrection as victory. Rather, the cross was the **victory won**, and the resurrection the **victory endorsed, proclaimed, and demonstrated**."[63] Instead of moving "beyond the Cross," as some suggest, we need to anchor our whole lives into the Cross of Christ and proclaim the **victory of the Cross** to the nations! Then we need to step out in Resurrection Power to reveal what Jesus did!

People sometimes question why, for forty years, have I stayed so committed to this one message? All I can say is—this is where I feel the fire. It's a heavy fiery passion and anointing, and it's always there with the message of the Cross and the Father's Cup.

David wrote me from California telling what happened when he preached in his home church. He said, "Every time I talked about the Cup in my sermon, I could feel my face burning. Honest, Dr. Sandy, I could feel the heat of the Holy Spirit burning against my skin!"

Over the years, I have heard this from former students and interns more times than I can count. Joshua, a former intern, was preaching about the Father's Cup in Nicaragua, when miracles started happening spontaneously. Deaf ears popped open, and a lady who was blind and paralyzed on one side of her body from the damage of a stroke, suddenly could see. In moments all the paralysis left her body.

Joshua said that whenever he preaches the Cross and the Father's Cup, people run to the altar weeping and crying, "Jesus, I didn't know!" "Thank you, Jesus for the Cross!" He said, "People later tell me that it's the message of the Cup that has never left them and has changed their lives forever."

So I hope you can see that this is not just my pet doctrine, or one of many streams. It's not another spoke in the wheel or another bandwagon on which to jump. Spurgeon said that just as all roads lead back to Rome, all sermons should lead back to the Cross. He cried, "Calvary preaching, Calvary theology, Calvary sermons! These are the things we want. And in proportion as we have Calvary exalted and Christ magnified, the gospel is preached."[64]

Most of all the Apostle Paul said, *"For I resolved to know nothing while I was with you except JESUS CHRIST AND HIM CRUCIFIED"* (1 Cor. 2:1-2). He said, *"The message of the CROSS . . . is the power of God"* (1 Cor. 1:18). He further said, *"Jews demand miraculous signs and Greeks look for wisdom, but we PREACH CHRIST CRUCIFIED"* (1 Cor. 1:23).

Paul's highest purpose was energized by this one electrifying cause in his life. With fierce passion he cried, *"God forbid that I should glory, save in the CROSS OF THE LORD JESUS CHRIST"* (Gal. 6:14).[65]

Paul was consumed with the glory of the Cross. He wrote, *"Christ's love COMPELS us because we are convinced that ONE DIED for all"* (2 Cor. 5:14). With all his heart he wanted to bring Jesus His reward.[66] He ministered in "the power outflowing from His resurrection" (Phil. 3:10, AMP), but it was because of the victory of the Cross.

## THE LAMB FOR THE NATIONS

Throughout this little book, I've weaved many stories of how the message of the Father's Cup is impacting nations. I do this so that—no matter where in the world you live—you will see how this message can shake your nation as well.

I'll never forget when Mary and Victor and I were ministering in Peru. One day I was teaching on the Father's Cup with a Spanish translator when I noticed the double doors in the back, which opened onto the street, kept blowing open and slamming against the inside walls. When ushers tried to close the doors, I said, "No, leave them open. Maybe someone will come in from the street to hear about the Lamb!"

I began pouring out the message of the Cup and the cry of dereliction, with a Spanish translator, and when the ministry concluded, a pastor came running up holding the hand of an elderly Jewish lady. This little Sephardic Jew had been walking down the street when she suddenly heard the sounds and the cries from the open door to the church. She slipped inside and when she heard what Jesus did for her, she ran up and found a pastor to interpret. In fast speaking Spanish, with tears running down her wrinkled face, she kept crying, "How can I find Jesus?"

We led her in a prayer to receive her Jewish Messiah, and she fell to the floor weeping under the power of God. I lifted my hands to heaven and cried, "Lamb of God, here is your reward!"

Our team of young revivalists brought this message of the Cross to India, sharing it through a nation with over one billion Hindus. We ministered in a pastor's conference and then I began teaching about the Father's Cup.

I noticed a very angry looking man, sitting on the third row, glaring at me with his arms folded. I later found out that he was the Superintendent of the Police Department in this large Indian City. He was Hindu and he had come to shut down the meeting if I dared to say anything negative about other religions. I was later told about one of our Brownsville students who had become a missionary to India. He preached against the false gods in India, and he had been thrown in jail. I didn't know this was illegal, and I *did* mention the false gods of Hinduism and other religions.

When I started showing a clip of Jesus being scourged from "The Passion of the Christ Movie" and then describing Jesus drinking the Father's Cup of wrath, I noticed the man started sweating profusely. Then I took a deep breath and roared out the cry of dereliction. I couldn't believe what happened next.

After a brief altar call, people rushed up to the front. The Police Superintendent rushed up too. But instead of shutting down the meeting and locking me in handcuffs, he cried out, ***"I want Jesus!"*** Seeing Jesus suffering, drinking the Father's Cup, and hearing the cry of Jesus from the Cross had melted his crusty heart and brought him to his knees.

When I returned to America, Bishop Samson, leader of over 4,000 churches in India, called and told me that the Police Superintendent brought his whole family to be baptized. "He has become my best church member!" said Dr. Samson. Then he said to me sincerely, "Dr. Sandy, all of India must hear this message of the Cross and the Father's Cup!" Sadly, however, when Covid 19 struck the world, Bishop Samson caught the disease and died. So we never got to go back and bring this message to the sincere and hungry people of India.

That's why I've written this little book. I've tried to keep it short and to focus it solely on the Father's Cup. My hope is that people, like the lady from Beijing, China, who trembled the whole time she translated it into Mandarin Chinese (see Introduction), can be inspired to translate it for their own people. I hope to translate it into as many Indian dialects and as many international languages as possible before I go to heaven. Oh, how I pray that God will raise *you* up to preach and teach this desperately needed message of *The Father's Cup!*

I stand back today and realize—it doesn't matter whether you are in South America or Mexico or Europe or Africa or China or India or any of the Asian countries, or North America, or any place else in the world—we all need to behold again the Crucified Lamb. We need to gaze into this blazing Cup until our hearts tremble and something inside us ignites with holy passion. Then we need to go out and tell everybody what Jesus did for them until this message spreads through our entire world!

So if you are hungry for this fire, not for your glory, but to bring glory to the Lamb, ask Him now:

> *Oh Jesus, with all my heart I bow before your Cross. With Paul I cry, "God forbid that I should*

*glory" except "in the cross of the Lord Jesus Christ" (Gal. 6:14). Let the fire of the Cross fall on me! Let the Resurrection Power consume me. Burn up everything in me that would taint your glory and let me live to bring glory to the Lamb for drinking the Father's Cup!*

Now we come to our last chapter as Jesus, the wounded Son, rushes through the halls of heaven and throws himself into the arms of His Abba. Watch the angels stand in holy awe as Father and Son embrace, weeping in each other's arms.

Listen now, as millions of holy angels cry, "Worthy is the Lamb!" But why do they say this? Why is He so worthy? Is it because of His miracles, His miraculous birth, His resurrection and ascension? The answer will surely cause your heart to tremble . . .

## Eight

# The Cry of Heaven

*"Worthy is the Lamb who was slain"*

One bright sunny day, Jesus leads His disciples up the Mount of Olives. Suddenly, He stops, lifts His hands, and "*while He was blessing them . . . He was carried up into heaven*" (Luke 24:51). As He rises, blessings drop from His lifted hands, as Spurgeon said, "the hands that bled now bless"[67]

Higher and higher He ascends, finally reaching the courts of heaven. Angels stand aghast, falling back in worship and awe. As He strides through the outer court, angelic beings see the deep wounds carved into His flesh. Jesus, however, is oblivious to their stares, for His eyes are focused up ahead.

Rushing onward, He sees the One He has longed to reach. There He is—*His Father*— waiting with arms outstretched and tears filling His eyes. Jesus finally reaches the throne room and falls into His arms, quietly sobbing. The Father's heart floods with love and longing. He has endured the separation from His Son with intense pain, but now at last His Wounded Son is home.

Waves of emotion break over the shores of their hearts. It's as though the loneliness of separation, the agony of the Father's Cup, the grief over the piercing pain of Jesus' cry— *"My God, why have You forsaken Me?"*—and the ecstasy of reunion all roll together in one swelling tide of overflowing feelings. They weep and weep in each other's arms.

All heaven hushes—not a sound, not a breath, only the muffled sobs of Father and Son. Timeless moments pass until finally, the Father opens His arms, takes a step back and points toward His Son. With love bursting from His heart, He thunders:

***BEHOLD THE LAMB, SLAIN FROM BEFORE THE CREATION OF THE WORLD! (see 1 Peter 1:20-21; Revelation 13:8).***

Now all of heaven explodes with joyful praise. Thousands upon thousands of angels explode with the cry of heaven: *"Worthy, Worthy, Worthy is the Lamb!"*

But why do they say He is worthy? Do they cry, "Worthy is the Lamb because of His divine Incarnation"? Do they cry "Worthy is the Lamb because of His amazing miracles and profound teachings"? Do they cry, "Worthy is the Lamb because of His glorious resurrection or ascension"? Do they cry, "Worthy is the Lamb because He taught us how to love"?

No. What do they say?

They humbly bow and cry with all the passion of heaven, *"You are worthy . . . because You were* ***SLAIN*** *and with Your* ***BLOOD*** *You purchased men for God from every tribe and tongue and people and nation"* (Rev. 5:9).

Do you see it? They are not praising His worthiness because He raised the dead or walked on water. They are not praising Him for His resurrection, His ascension, or even His magnificent glory. They aren't even praising Him for His wonderful blessings. They are praising Him for **His sacrifice at Calvary** which reaches its zenith when He engulfed ***the Father's Cup.***

And because of this, all they can do is humbly bow and cry **worthy is the Lamb!**

This is why our cry on earth and heaven is—**"THE LAMB WHO WAS SLAIN IS WORTHY TO RECEIVE THE REWARD OF HIS SUFFERING!"**

## WHERE ARE THE APOSTLES AND PREACHERS?

In several of my books, I've been asking—Where are the apostles, like Paul, who will glory in the Cross, who will preach only *"Christ and Him crucified,"* and who will change the whole world with this message? Where are the apostles, like

Peter, who will preach the apostolic message of the Cross until people are *"pierced to the heart"* with the gospel (Acts 2:37)?[68]

Where are the prophets, like John the Baptist, who will focus on the central message and cry —*"Behold the Lamb of God"?* If indeed *"the testimony of Jesus is the spirit of prophecy"* (Rev. 19:10), then where are the prophets who will show us JESUS when they prophesy? Where are the visionaries like the Apostle John who will behold the Lamb on the throne and bring the revelation through his writings down to earth? Where are the evangelists, like Philip with the Ethiopian Eunuch (Acts 8:25-40), who will explain the Scriptures about the Cross in Isaiah 53 to lost and dying souls?

Where are the teachers and preachers who will look into the garden of Gethsemane and tell the story with such passion that people can feel the fire and fall on their faces before God? Where are those in this generation who will bring forth the Lamb, through books or art or music or drama or movies? Where are the young ones who will bring this message into the digital age?

The good news is this— ***it is* happening!** Think of the amazing Christian movies like: "I Can Only Imagine," or "The Jesus Revolution," or "The Chosen." Think of all the glorious songs about the Lamb today which seem to open heaven and show us the glory of the Lamb above. What about the Ministry Schools that fill YouTube with phenomenal worship like Jesus Image or Bethel School of Ministry. I think of the passionate young preachers who came out of Brownsville Revival School of Ministry or Fire School or even came out of our camp in

Alabama. God is moving in the young generation today and it is marvelous to behold.

And think of the phenomena of campus baptisms sweeping the nation as thousands of young adults give their lives to Christ and submit to public baptisms in pools and lakes and oceans and rivers and fountains. God seems to be raising up Christian young people to counter the anti-Semitic rallies on other campuses and who will lead the way in the coming Revival.

I think also of young fathers and mothers who are producing solid, Christ-centered homes for their children. It's not necessarily about preaching a fiery sermon on a microphone. It's also about raising up Godly families to strengthen the Church and the backbone of this nation. It's not just about having a burning heart; it's about having a burning life. It's about the character of Christ being etched within your soul. It's about the love, the humility, the kindness, the holiness which exemplifies the way of the Cross and spills out to your whole family.

## SUICIDE BROKEN BY A LOOK AT THE CUP

Thomas left our spring "Unquenchable Flame Internship" in Alabama, absolutely bursting with the message of the Father's Cup. Everywhere he went—to the ticket agent in the airport, to the passenger next to him on the plane, to his wife, to the boss at work—he cried, "Do you know about *the Father's Cup?*" Of course, they all said "No!" so he opened up his heart and began gushing out the beautiful, painful, glorious story of *the Father's Cup.*

One night he was invited to preach in a little church, and, of course, he preached about the Father's Cup. The Lord showed him someone there was struggling with suicide. Before he started his message, he gave the word about suicide and then launched into his description of the Father's Cup. At the end of the meeting a former Muslim, who had been saved at Teen Challenge, came forward to admit, "I am that man. I have been planning to hang myself tonight because I'm so depressed."

The man paused to wipe away a tear and then said excitedly, "But when you described the Father's Cup of eternal wrath roaring down on Jesus—in my place— I realized that He took all my mistakes, all my shame, all my regrets, all my past sins on himself and He was punished for me. And suddenly, I could feel the spirit of suicide and depression lifting off of me—all because *Jesus drank the Cup for me!"*

Oh, do you see? If we can show people what Jesus did for them by drinking the Father's Cup and taking the punishment of hell that they deserve, they can receive hope. How can I drown in depression because my life is falling apart—*when Jesus drank the Cup to overcome all my grief and pain?* (see Is. 53:3-4).

How can I still hold on to sin or get bitter Hwhen I'm rejected, criticized, or falsely accused, for *Jesus drank the Father's Cup!* How can I withhold forgiveness when Jesus poured out every drop of His sacred blood to wash away my bitterness and take the wrath for the one who wounded me?

How can I blame God for my pain? How can I ever think God has forsaken me— *Jesus drank the Father's Cup* all alone. He was forsaken for me, so that I would never be forsaken by God! Even if someone I love dies, I can be grateful that He defeated death and made a way for my loved one to enter heaven—because He *drank the Father's Cup!*

Yes, this is what's been missing from our lives, but most of all it has been missing from the Church. How can we blame God for human suffering, when He gave His beautiful Son to take the ultimate suffering? The pinnacle of human suffering is the hell He endured when He drank *the Father's Cup!*

How then can we withhold our hearts from Him . . .

How can we stay lukewarm any longer . . .

How can we be too shy to witness . . .

How can we avoid helping the poor . . .

How can we stand on the sidelines and overlook the current harvest of souls and the great coming Revival . . .

How can we do anything but passionately keep the fire of the gospel in the center of Revival . . .

And when Revival fires burn, how can we do anything but embrace the Cross and give Jesus every ounce of the glory He deserves.

## LASTING REVIVAL

Yes, Revival is in the very air we breathe today. And once we open our hearts to the full glorious work of Christ at Calvary, it will open the way for lasting Revival.

Think about this often-overlooked verse, which Jesus spoke: *"I have come to **cast fire** upon the earth,"* and He is speaking here of the fire of Revival. Then He says, *"But I have a **baptism** to undergo, and how distressed I am until it is accomplished"* (Luke 12:49-50).

Jesus endured His **baptism of fire** when He drank the Father's Cup of everlasting wrath and hell. And because He paid such a price, now He wants to give us a **baptism of the Holy Spirit and FIRE!**

He promised He would set the world ablaze with Revival. Revival is the Resurrection Power that Jesus died to give us. He drank the Father's Cup so that this Resurrection Power can fill the Church and flow to all the earth!

Yes, He will indeed ignite His Church again. He will awaken His slumbering Bride, like He awakened His disciples in the garden. God will cast fire on His Church, which is the fire of Revival, just like He promised.

You see, even as a river flows back to its source in the ocean, the Revival God is sending will lead us back to the ocean of God in the heart of the Lamb. *"For from Him, and through Him, and to Him are all things"* (Rom. 11:36). Even as the final book of the Bible gives a revelation of the Lamb, the final great

Revival will bring a REVELATION OF THE LAMB. It will be a Revival **of** the Lamb, **for** the Lamb, **through** the Lamb, and **back to** the Lamb.

Now He calls you to be His mouth piece, sounding abroad the message of the Cross, the Cup, the Blood, and the risen Lamb—*the complete Gospel.* He calls each of us to do our part to set the world ablaze by sharing the good news of the gospel—the true, pure, and "*eternal gospel*" of Jesus Christ (see Rev. 14:6).[69]

And even if the whole earth shakes, we need not fear, for *Jesus drank the Father's Cup!* That's why, we have an anchor. We have unshakable ground on which to stand. We have an unquenchable hope in the midst of any storm. Why? Because *Jesus drank the Father's Cup!*

## HE IS WORTHY

Stephen, a leader in YWAM and a former leader here at the camp, ministered to missionaries in the Philippines. His wife, Leah, said he had never seen anything like what happened. Because ISIS had taken over this area in the island and had established Sharia Law, it was extremely dangerous for Christians, even to the point of being kidnapped and even possibly beheaded. Stephen had to be hidden undercover when not ministering.

But despite the danger, Stephen would not retreat. He poured out his heart about the Father's Cup of eternal wrath thundering down on Jesus in wave after wave of punishment. He bellowed Jesus' cry, *"My God, why have you forsaken Me?"* He described His glorious resurrection, and he painted the picture as passionately and graphically as he could. Then something amazing happened.

Suddenly, spontaneously, the missionaries who had come from all over the world, lifted their hands and erupted in extravagant worship. On and on they cried. With earnest passion they exploded, *"WORTHY, WORTHY, WORTHY IS THE LAMB!"*

All Stephen could do was sit down, cover his face, and sob. With all his heart he knew that Jesus, the Lamb who was slain, was receiving His reward.

You see, there is an expulsive uproar waiting to erupt from a unified Church. From every *"tribe and tongue and people and nation,"* the cry of heaven will explode.

What is that cry? It's the cry of angels, living creatures, and twenty-four elders all bursting out with one magnificent crescendo: *"WORTHY, WORTHY, WORTHY IS THE LAMB!"*

## NOW DO YOU KNOW HOW MUCH HE LOVES YOU?

Jesus loved you so much it hurt. You see, you can never understand how much He loves you until you truly know what He did for you on the Cross. He loved you so deeply He couldn't bear to be apart from you. That's why He drank the Father's

Cup. He engulfed ever drop of your punishment so that you could be forgiven and live with Him forever.

Now, with a heart full of gratitude, will you pray this prayer sincerely:

*Oh, Jesus, You drank the Cup for me! You shed every drop of Your blood for Me! Oh, my God, I can never thank You enough for giving Your Son to drink the Father's Cup! It astounds me that You would take the Son of Your heart and pour Your Cup of wrath on Him. If I had a million tongues, I could never praise You enough! If I had a trillion years to worship, it would never be long enough!*

*So, shake the Church, shake my nation, and shake this world until all creation cries, "WORTHY, WORTHY, WORTHY IS THE LAMB!" For a billion reasons You are worthy, but most of all You are WORTHY because you hung on a Cross and drank every drop of the Father's Cup!*

And now, as you prepare to lay this book aside, lift your gaze to heaven to behold the wounded Lamb seated on the throne (see Rev. 5:9). With the angels, join their song as you cry with all your heart:

***"THE LAMB WHO WAS SLAIN IS WORTHY TO RECEIVE THE REWARD OF HIS SUFFERING!"***[70]

*Now, Lord Jesus, I offer this little book back to You. It was on my birthday, many years ago, that You first spoke to me about writing this simple book, concentrating primarily on the Father's Cup and telling some of the stories from other nations that resulted from this message. Now I just turned 81 years old, and I am offering back to You this third edition of this priceless message. I pray You will breathe on these pages and on every person who reads them.*

*And to everyone who has read this book: I want you to know that I am extremely grateful to you for taking your time to focus on this vital message. I pray that the Lord will lay His hand upon you now and impart to you the Holy Spirit and FIRE. I pray He will raise you up to bring glory to the Lamb who was slain, for what He suffered for you. And because you have dared to look into the Father's Cup, may your heart NEVER, EVER STOP TREMBLING with passion and love for the Lamb!*

# Endnotes

## Introduction: Do You Tremble?

1. I've written many books which tell about the Father's Cup, but this time I knew the Lord wanted me to write a book which focuses solely on the Cup. It must be short, burning, and to the point. The primary reason for this brevity is so that it can be easily translated into other languages. The story I told in this Introduction about the translator from Beijing, China reveals the fruit of that decision. When I ministered in Hong Kong several years ago, the communists were not cracking down on Christians like they do today. Now I am so grateful to God that this unknown Chinese lady translated this book and has made it available to the underground church in China.

2. The Cross is the centrality of the whole Bible. Everything leads up to it and flows out from it, as J. C. Ryle said, "If you have not yet found that Christ crucified is the foundation of the whole volume, you have read your Bible hitherto to very little profit. Your religion is a heaven without a sun...a compass without a needle, a clock without spring or weights, a lamp without oil" (J. C. Ryle, "The Cross of Christ" [1816 – 1900]).

3. Some would argue, *But Jesus is no longer on the Cross, so we shouldn't look at Him bleeding and dying at Calvary.* Paul would disagree. When describing his preaching to the Galatians, he said, *"Before your very EYES Jesus Christ was clearly portrayed as CRUCIFIED"* (Gal. 3:1). Since the Galatians were not at the Cross, it follows that Paul described Christ crucified in his preaching. However, we must always keep the Resurrection connected to the message of Calvary. To leave out the Resurrection is to give only half of the gospel. We must have the fullness of both.

4. Though the "Cup" is normally not capitalized, I am capitalizing it in this book for emphasis. Also I am taking the liberty to capitalize the Cross.

## Chapter 1: A Blood-Soaked Prayer

5. W. E. Vine, *Vine's Expository Dictionary of Old and New Testament Words* (Nashville, TN: Thomas Nelson Publishers, 1996), p. 185. Remember that Luke was a physician, and he used the medical term in the Greek: *thrombos*, which he knew meant clots of blood.

6. Jonathan Edwards, *"Christ's Agony," The Works of Jonathan Edwards*, Vol. I (Edinburgh, Scotland: Banner of Truth Trust, 1995), p. 868.

7. C.H. Spurgeon, "Gethsemane," *Spurgeon's Sermons on the Death and Resurrection of Jesus* (Peabody, MS: Hendrickson Publishers, 2005), p. 128.

8. Spurgeon, "The Agony of Gethsemane," *Twelve Sermons on the Passion and Death of Christ* (Grand Rapids, MI: Baker Book House, 1971), p. 10.

9. Arthur W. Pink, *The Seven Sayings of the Savior on the Cross* (Grand Rapids, MI: Baker Book House, 1958), p. 74.

10. Jonathan Edwards, "Christ's Agony," p. 868.

11. Jonathan Edwards was the leader of America's First Great Awakening and considered one of America's greatest theologians. Therefore, the fact that he would say that Jesus came, above all, to drink the Father's Cup, should cause us to realize the profound importance of this Cup. Why then do we fail to mention it in our gospel messages?

12. The Gospel writers—Matthew, Mark, Luke, and John—all wrote about this Cup when they described Jesus' prayer in the garden. The Lord settled it when He said to Peter, *"Put your sword away! Shall I not drink* ***the CUP the Father*** *has given Me?"* (John 18:11). But most of all, Jesus sealed the colossal significance of this Cup when He soaked his prayer in **His own blood!**

13. The book to which Kathy Strandjorn was referring was my book *UNDONE by a Revelation of the Lamb* (Creation House, 2013). Order from any Christian bookstore or our website: www.beholdthelamb.org

## Chapter 2: What is the Cup

14. Thomas Goodwin cited in C.H. Spurgeon, *Spurgeon's Sermons on the Death and Resurrection of Jesus,* (Peabody, MA: Hendrickson Publishers, Inc., 2005), p. 122.

15. John R. W. Stott, *The Cross of Christ* (Downers Grove, IL: InterVarsity Press, 1987), p. 77.

16. Alfred Edersheim says that the temple opened at midnight in the days of Jesus of Nazareth (Alfred Edersheim, *The Life and Times of Jesus the Messiah,* Book V [Grand Rapids, MI: Wm. B. Eerdmans Publishing Co., 1976], p. 508).

17. Professor Wayne Grudem, in his massive and wonderful *Systematic Theology,* says, "Theologians speak of . . . a covenant that is not between God and man, but is among the members of the Trinity." He explains, "This covenant they call 'the covenant of redemption.' It is an agreement among the Father, Son, and Holy Spirit, in which the Son agreed to become a man, be our representative, obey the commands of the covenant of works on our behalf and pay the penalty for sin, which we deserved" (Wayne Grudem, *Systematic Theology* [Leicester, England: Inter-Varsity Press, 1994], p. 518).

18. "This Old Testament imagery will have been well known to Jesus," writes John R. W. Stott (*The Cross of Christ* [Downers Grove, IL: InterVarsity Press, 1986], p. 77). Other scriptures on the Cup of wrath: Job 6:4, 21:20; Isaiah 51:17-22, Isaiah 53:3-5,10; Jeremiah 25:15-29, 49:12; Ezekiel 23:32-34; Habakkuk 2:16; Revelation 14:10, 16:1

19. Though some hold the misconception that this was only a "cup of suffering," which meant Jesus' physical and emotional pain, John Stott says that such a concept is "ludicrous." Stott explains that "the cup from which He shrank . . . symbolized neither the physical pain of being flogged and crucified, nor the mental distress of being despised and rejected even by His own people, but rather the spiritual agony of bearing the sins of the world . . . and enduring the divine judgment which those sins deserved" (John Stott, *Cross of Christ*, p. 76).

20. Jonathan Edwards, "The History of the Work of Redemption,"

*The Works of Jonathan Edwards,* Vol. 1 (Edinburgh: Banner of Truth Trust, 1995), p. 546.

21. The Bible doesn't indicate that Abraham carried the fire in a cup, but he would not have carried this fire in his bare hand, so it follows that the fire would be carried in a pail or cup. See Leviticus 1 for the preparation of a lamb for the burnt offering. For a beautiful chapter on Abraham and Isaac's sacrifice, see my new book *MASHIACH,* which shows how a Revelation of the Lamb reveals the Jewish Messiah. Order from Amazon or our website: www.beholdthelamb.org/bookstore

22. Holocaust offering: *Holo* means "whole" and *caust* means "burnt," (*NIV study Bible,* footnote on Leviticus 1:3).

23. Edwards explained that Jesus needed to see what he was about to endure if he surrendered fully to drinking the Cup: "Christ was going to be cast into a dreadful furnace of wrath, and it was not proper that He should plunge Himself into it blindfolded, by not knowing how dreadful the furnace was. Therefore, that He might know what was in this cup . . . God brought the cup that He was to drink and set it down before Him that He might have a full view of it and see what it was before He took it and drank it" (Jonathan Edwards, "Christ's Agony," p. 867).

24. R.C. Sproul, "Since Jesus Took Our Punishment, Why Didn't He Need to Go to Hell?" video, Ligonier Ministries, September 14, 2020, Internet: https://www.google.com/search?q=did+christ+descend+into+hell+ligonier.

25. Charles Spurgeon, "It is Finished," *The Power of the Cross of Christ,* Lance Wubbels, comp. (Lynnwood, WA: Emerald Books, 1995), p. 141. Jonathan Edwards, "Christ's Agony," pp. 868, 871.

26. A. W. Pink, *Seven Sayings of Jesus on the* Cross (Grand Rapids, MI: Baker Book House, 1958), p. 72.

27. John Stott, *The Cross of Christ,* p. 79.

28. Jonathan Edwards, "Christ's Agony," p. 869.

29. Jesus warned, *"He who believes in the Son has eternal life; but he who does not obey the Son will not see life, but the* ***wrath of***

***God** abides on him"* (John 3:36). Yet, sadly, in our politically correct, postmodern era, the concept of hell is mocked. Though Jesus spoke often of hell, people today doubt its very existence. And yet, if we don't understand the reality of hell, we won't understand the depths to which our Savior went to save us when He drank the Father's Cup. We won't understand the magnitude of His love. Please do not be deceived by the heretical view that because of the Cross, we now need no longer repent for sin. If we sin, "the blood of Jesus His Son cleanses us from all unrighteousness" (1 John 1:7), but only if we confess our sins (1 John 1:9).

## Chapter 3: Amazing Love

30. In fact, everything He did in the garden, said Edwards, was "from the strong love that was in His heart. His tears that flowed from his eyes were from love; His great sweat was from love; his blood and His prostrating himself on the ground before the Father, was from love. His earnest crying to God was from the strength and ardency of His love" (Jonathan Edwards, "Christ's Agony," cited in edited version in *The Unquenchable Flame,* p. 221).

31. Ibid.

32. Charles Wesley, "And Can It Be?" (1738).

33. Jonathan Edwards, "Christ's Agony," edited version in Sandy D. Kirk, *The Unquenchable Flame* (Shippensburg, PA: Destiny Image, 2012), p. 196.

34. Wayne Grudem, *Systematic Theology* [Leicester, England: Inter-Varsity Press, 1994], p. 575.

35. Colby Itkowitz, *The Washington Post,* "The Fearless Father who Threw himself on a Suicide Bomber, Saving 'hundreds' of Lives in Beirut," November 16, 2015. This happened the day before the massacre in central Paris in 2015, so it was largely overlooked by the mainstream media.

36. Eugene Bach, *Back to Jerusalem* (Lumberton, MS: Back to Jerusalem, 2014), pp. 5-6.

## Chapter 4: Punished for Me!

37. Charles Spurgeon, "The Three Hours of Darkness," *The Power of the Cross of Christ*, p. 95.

38. Even as the Israelites were healed from the serpent's venom as they looked at the brass serpent on the pole (Numb. 21), sin loses its grip when we gaze deeply at the Lamb on the pole of the Cross Spurgeon said, "Beloved, if you long to conquer sin within you, behold the Lamb of God!" (Charles H. Spurgeon, "Behold the Lamb," *Spurgeon's Encyclopedia of Sermons,* Vol 2 [Baker Book House, 1977], p. 113. Jesus described hell as a place of *"outer darkness where there will be weeping and gnashing of teeth"* (Matt. 8:12), but, as John Stott wrote, "into that outer darkness the Son of God plunged for us" (John Stott, *The Cross of Christ,* p. 79). It is not God's desire to send us to hell, but when we reject the great gift of His one and only Son, continuing on in sin, our sin sends us to hell!

39. Jim Chern, "Crucifixion of Indifference," *Homily on the Spot*, August 3, 2024, homilyonthespot.com.

40. Pastor Wickenol said, "When I came here, I was crying to God, 'Do it in me!' Then I repented for never feeling Christ's pain. I opened my heart and Jesus began to squeeze it. Now I have the Cup message in my life, and I feel fire!" Pastor Joseph said, "When I took my courses in Bible College, the Cross was never mentioned. Now I burn to tell about the fire of the Cross! I know I will set my church ablaze and all of Kenya!" Pastor George said, "I could preach before but not like this. Now power comes out when I preach the Cup and the Cross. Souls are saved and people are slain by the message. This fire will save Kenya!"

41. God has used Sophie and her mum Nicky McLachlan from England and her Awaken Love team, who have helped develop this beautiful orphanage outside Kisumu, Kenya: see www.awakenlove.org.uk.

## Chapter 5: The Cry of the Ages

42. Luther wrote that all theology should be developed "within earshot of the dying cry of Jesus" (Jürgen Moltmann, *The Crucified*

*God: The Cross of Christ as the Foundation and Criticism of Christian Theology* [Minneapolis, Minnesota, 1993], p. 201). John Piper says, "This is the cry of the damned, and He was damned for us!" (John Piper, "Ask Pastor John," Episode 805, March 1, 2016).

43. If we really knew the destructiveness of sin, we would never let the politically correct culture twist us into its mold. Sin destroys the human soul. Sin opens us to demonic attack. Sin decays the human heart. Sin blinds our eyes to truth. Sin sears our tender conscience. Sin deceives, and most of all sin blocks us from the presence of God: *"Your iniquities have made a separation between you and your God, and your sins have hidden His face from you so that He does not hear"* (Is. 59:2). Even more, sin crucified our precious Lord Jesus!

44. Charles Spurgeon, "It Is Finished!" *Power of the Cross,* p. 141.

45. Charles Spurgeon said, "The words 'It is finished!' consolidated heaven, shook hell, comforted earth, delighted the Father, glorified the Son, brought down the Spirit and confirmed the everlasting covenant to all the chosen seed" (Spurgeon, *The Power of the Cross*, Lance Wubbels, comp. "It Is Finished!" p. 145).

## Chapter 6: Pierced

46. Jesus doesn't release himself to hell for a fictitious battle with Satan. He doesn't say from the Cross, "It is *almost* finished." He *does* say, "It is finished!" He doesn't cry, "Satan, into your hands I commit My spirit." He cries, "Father, into Your hands I commit My spirit." Peter tells us he proclaims His victory in hades (1 Pet. 3:19; 4:6), but hades is not hell. The victory was won on the Cross, NOT IN HELL. This is a heresy that has plagued the church and diminished our understanding of the victory of the Cross. Please see my book *UNDONE* or *The Unquenchable Flame* for further explanation: www.beholdthelamb.org/bookstore or Wayne Grudem's *Systematic Theology* book.

47. Physiologically, what actually caused His death? It was not from blood loss, asphyxiation, or sword thrust, but from the rupturing of His own heart. What then caused His heart to rupture? It was from the agony of drinking—*all alone*—the Father's Cup.

48. Dr. Truman Davis states, "There was an escape of watery fluid from the sac surrounding the heart and the blood of the interior of the heart. This is another conclusive postmortem evidence that Jesus died, not the usual death of crucifixion death by suffocation, but of heart failure due to shock and constriction of the heart by fluid in the pericardium" (C. Truman Davis, "A Physician's Look at the Crucifixion" *Arizona Medicine*, Vol. 22, No. 3, March 1965). Leon Morris adds, "William Stroud wrote that it meant a physically ruptured heart, with the result that 'the blood separates into its constituent parts so as to present the appearance commonly termed blood and water'" (Leon Morris, *Reflections on the Gospel of John* [Peabody, MA: Hendrickson Publishers, Inc., 2000], pp. 674-675).

49. This love wound is bittersweet. It brings sorrow at first because it causes sincere repentance, but it is ultimately a glorious wound. It causes one to fall more deeply in love with Jesus. It fills the heart with a trembling fire, an aching love, a burning passion for the Lamb.

50. For a beautiful, heart-wrenching novel, which tells the story of Yeshua (Jesus) and His own mother at the Cross, read my book *MASHIACH, Finding Your Jewish Messiah through a Revelation of the Lamb.* It also comes in an audio book. Order from Amazon of www.beholdthelamb.org.

51. Charles Spurgeon, *Spurgeon's Expository Encyclopedia*, Vol. 8, "How Hearts Are Softened," (Grand Rapids: Baker Book House, 1977), p. 377.

52. We often pray, "O God, *'rend the heavens and come down!'*" (Is. 64:1), but we need to pray "O God, rend **my heart**!" Author Peter Madden says, "the reality and extent of revival depend on the depth of the incision of the Cross of Christ in the heart" (Peter J. Madden, *The Secret of Wigglesworth's Power* [New Kensington, PA: Whittaker House, 2000], p. 66).

53. A. B. Simpson, "The Brand of the Cross;" cited in A. W. Tozer, *The Radical Cross: Living the Passion of Christ* (Camp Hill, PA: Wingspread Publishers, 2009), p. 140.

54. Peter Madden explains: "We are just like the temple in Jerusalem at the time of crucifixion. As the thick veil of the temple was completely

torn in two, through the awesome power of the Cross (Luke 23:45), so must this same power tear apart the thick veil of the natural order within us, for we are the temple of God" (Peter Madden, *The Secret of Wigglesworth's Power*, p. 64).

55. G. Campbell Morgan said, "It is the crucified man that can preach the cross. Said Thomas, 'except I shall see in his hands the print of the nails . . . I will not believe.' Dr. Parker said that what Thomas said of Christ, the world is saying about the church. And the world is also saying to every preacher: Unless I see in your hands the print of the nails, I will not believe. It is true. It is the man . . . who has died with Christ, . . . that can preach the cross of Christ" (G. Campbell Morgan, *Evangelism* (Henry E. Walter, 1964) pp. 59-60; cited in John R. W. Stott, *The Cross of Christ,* p. 351).

56. Father's Day 1995 was the day the Holy Spirit used Evangelist Steve Hill and swept through John Kilpatrick's Church in Pensacola. This was known as the Brownsville Revival, which drew over four million people from around the world to the Brownsville Assembly of God Church. Long lines of people would camp out all day, waiting for the doors to open at 6:00 p.m. I had the privilege of teaching seven courses in the Brownsville Revival School of Ministry and it was wonderful.

57. Dietrich Bonhoeffer, the great German theologian who was hung to death for being involved in trying to rid Germany of Hitler, said that "only one thing is of importance" to the one who truly wants God: "He wants to see God; he wants to hear God; he wants to receive God; he wants to know God. He wants . . . nothing else like he wants God . . . There is no easy way to God for He resides behind the Cross" (Geffrey B. Kelly and F. Burton Nelson, eds. *A Testament to Freedom: The Essential Writings of Dietrich Bonhoeffer* [San Francisco: Harper, 1990], pp. 210, 116).

## Chapter 7: Resurrection Power

58. The Hebrew word *rahap* means to tremble, shake, or hover, Hebrew Dictionary, #8173, *The Hebrew-Greek Study Bible* (Chattanooga, TN: AMG Publishers, 1996), p. 8120.

59. The Reason we know that the Holy Spirit lifted from Jesus is because of His cry from the Cross: "Eloi, Eloi, lama sabachthani" (Mark 15:34). The name "Eloi" is plural, showing that He was crying to Father and Spirit of God.

60. Charles Spurgeon, *2200 Quotations from the Writings of Charles Spurgeon,* Tom Carter, comp. (Grand Rapids, MI: Baker Book House, 1988), p. 200.

61. Jonathan Edwards, "Christ's Agony," p. 867.

62. Martin Luther's famous 95 Theses included strong emphasis on the true Gospel. See my new book, *Pierced to the Heart with the Gospel,* Second Edition, order from Amazon or our website: www.beholdthelamb.org. A. W. Tozer said, "It may take nothing short of a **new reformation to restore the Cross** to its right place in the theology and life of the Church" (A. W. Tozer, "The Cross is a Radical Thing," *The Radical Cross* [Camp Hill, PA: Wingspread Publishers, 2005], p. 5).

63. Now, in our day, people seem to want to hear preaching on prosperity and power and personal identity and success. But the truth is the greatest power of all is hidden in the Cross. Paul said, *"The message of the cross . . . is the power of God"* (1 Corinthians 1:18). The Cross is the hiding place of God's true power. It is where authentic fire—not "strange fire"—can be found. See Leviticus 10-11 and my book *Unquenchable Flame.*

64. C. H. Spurgeon, *2200 Quotations from the Writings of C.H. Spurgeon,* Tom Carter, comp. (Grand Rapids, MI: Baker Book House, 1988), p. 46.

65. Charles Spurgeon made this brilliant comment about this verse: "He could have gloried in the incarnation: angels sang of it, wise men came from the far East to behold it . . . . He might have gloried in the life of Christ: was there ever such another, so benevolent and blameless? He might have gloried in the resurrection of Christ: it is the world's great hope concerning those that are asleep. He might have gloried in our Lord's ascension: for He *'led captivity captive,'* and all His followers glory in His victory . . . .Yet the apostle selected beyond all these that center of the Christian system, that point which is most assailed by

its foes, that focus of the world's derision —the cross" (Spurgeon, *The Passion and Death of Christ*, "The Cross Our Glory," p. 143)

66. One day Paul ventured into Athens, where men prided themselves on vain philosophies. Here he learned a valuable lesson. Though he preached an eloquent sermon at the famous Areopagus, he didn't mention the Cross of Christ in his sermon (Acts 17:22-31). Some scholars refer to this as a model sermon, but don't overlook the fact that only *"a few men became followers of Paul"* in Athens (17:34). By the time he came to nearby Corinth, I believe he was broken and done with human eloquence. I believe this is why he said to the Corinthians, *"I did not come with eloquence or superior wisdom as I proclaimed to you the testimony about God. For I resolved to know nothing while I was with you except JESUS CHRIST AND HIM CRUCIFIED"* (I Cor. 2:2).

67. Charles Spurgeon, "Our Lord's Attitude in Ascension," *Spurgeon's Expository Encyclopedia,* Vol. 4.

68. See Leon Morris, *The Apostolic Preaching of the Cross* (Grand Rapids, MI: Wm. B. Eerdmans Publishing Co., 1955).

69. Paul defined the gospel as the death, burial, and resurrection of Jesus Christ (see 1 Cor. 15:1-4). He also said, "I am not ashamed of the gospel of Christ for it is the power of God unto salvation" (Romans 1:16).

70. This cry was given to the Church by Ludwig von Zinzendorf and the Moravians in the 1700s. The first time I ever read these words, I was forever gripped by the truth they carry.

# Dr. Sandy's Books

*(Translations in 9 languages)*

***MASHIACH*** (2024) Discovering your Jewish Messiah through a REVELATION OF THE LAMB. Audio book of *The Mystery of Avraham's Lamb* (currently *Finding Mashiach)*

***UNDONE by a Revelation of the Lamb***, (2013) This is Dr. Sandy's premier book, unveiling the glory of the Lamb before creation, through the Bible, and on into eternity. Save money by ordering *Undone* on our website.

**Basic Workbook** for *UNDONE*

**Advanced Workbook** for *UNDONE*

***Pierced to the Heart by the Gospel*** (2022) boldly calls the Church back to the pure Gospel. Discover the Gospel secrets of Wesley, Whitefield, Jonathan Edwards, Charles Spurgeon, Billy Graham, Reinhard Bonnke; Steve Hill, John Kilpatrick, and a new generation of gospel preachers today.

***Do You Tremble?*** (2021) This is a second edition of *The Father' Cup* but it also includes the sermon by Jonathan Edwards, which first opened Dr. Sandy's eyes to this cup.

***The Father's Cup*** (2016) Third edition. Gaze into the blazing contents of the cup which Jesus prayed about in the garden and drank on Calvary. Translated into the African dialect. Audio book on ***The Father's Cup***

***India Ablaze*** (2016) The glory of the Lamb for India, translated into Hindi, Talagu, Malayalam, and Tamil

***Louada*** (2022) a heart-warming story of hope. How a broken little abused girl overcame her pain and became an anointed minister of the gospel.

**Mama Hazel** (2017) A powerful story of one woman's amazing faith

***Bethlehem's Lamb*** (2011) The glory of the Incarnation of Jesus Christ. **Audio book of *Bethlehem's Lamb***

***The Masterpiece*** (2009) Viewing the crucifixion, resurrection and ascension through the Apostle John's eyes. Audio book available

***The Glory of the Lamb*** (2005) The eternal glory of the Lamb of God, an abbreviated version of *Undone*. Translated into German, Spanish, and Philippine dialect.

***The Glory of the Lamb* DVD series** (a set of five DVDs)

***The Unquenchable Flame*** (2010) How to keep revival flames burning by keeping the lamb upon the altar. Translated into German.

***Rivers of Glory*** (2006) Healing a young generation through the river that flows from the side of the Lamb

***A Revelation of the Lamb for America*** (2005) After the fall of the Twin Towers on 9-11, America desperately needs a revelation of the Lamb. Filled with stories of patriotic heroes that show us our greatest Hero—Jesus Christ.

***America Ablaze*** (2004) Revival history with emphasis on revival for a young generation

***Reaching Your Son's Heart*** (2022) Healing the orphan spirit through the power of Calvary love.

***America's Broken Boys*** (2021) 3 powerful steps for mending the relationship between a father and his son

**Dad, Where Are You?** (2021) Healing wounded young people of their father wounds through the power of Jesus' sacrifice.

(3rd edition). Translated into Spanish. ***The Pierced Generation*** (2013, first edition) How a generation of wounded young adults can be healed at Calvary.

***Healing A Wounded Heart*** (2021) Five steps for healing your wounded heart

**A Guidebook for Women's Aglow:** (2018) **How to Heal a Wounded Generation**

***Wiping the Tears on the Soul of America*** (2016) Healing Racial Wounds through repentance, forgiveness, and love

***The Wounded Soldier*** (2015) Healing wounded hearts of veterans through the power of Calvary's love. Free to veterans.
**Audio book on *The Wounded Soldier***

***The Pain in an African Heart*** (2012) Healing African Wounds

***The Pain*** (2021) Healing the pain in a Teenager's heart

## FAMILY BOOKS

***Bethlehem's Lamb Series* (full color illustrated Christmas book series for the whole family),** (2023)

**Book 1: *The Nativity Story for the Whole Family***

**Book 2: *God's Grand Love Story***

**Book 3: The Savior of the World is Born**

*This series is for you to read to your family; it is for all ages at Christmas time. It is fully illustrated by Dr. Sandy.*

## CHILDREN'S BOOKS

***Would Jesus Eat His Vegetables?***

***How Would Jesus Act at Bedtime?***

***Would Jesus Be a Bad Sport?***

Order any of these books from www.beholdthelamb.org website bookstore. Many of them are also on Amazon.

# About the Author

Dr. Sandy earned a Master of Science in Secondary Education, a Master of Arts in theology, and a Ph.D. from Fuller Theological Seminary, receiving the coveted "Contextualization Award" for her Ph.D. dissertation. She has taught in Bible Schools around the world and directed a camp and retreat center for 22 years. She is a best-selling author and has written and published over thirty-four books. She has three wonderful children and two amazing grandchildren

Made in the USA
Middletown, DE
21 January 2025